The Practice of Person-C
and Family Th

The Practice of Person-Centred Couple and Family Therapy

Charles J. O'Leary

palgrave
macmillan

First published 2012 by
PALGRAVE MACMILLAN

Palgrave Macmillan in the UK is an imprint of Macmillan Publishers Limited, registered in England, company number 785998, of Houndmills, Basingstoke, Hampshire RG21 6XS.

Palgrave Macmillan in the US is a division of St Martin's Press LLC, 175 Fifth Avenue, New York, NY 10010.

Palgrave Macmillan is the global academic imprint of the above companies and has companies and representatives throughout the world.

Palgrave® and Macmillan® are registered trademarks in the United States, the United Kingdom, Europe and other countries

ISBN-13: 978–0–230–23318–8

This book is printed on paper suitable for recycling and made from fully managed and sustained forest sources. Logging, pulping and manufacturing processes are expected to conform to the environmental regulations of the country of origin.

A catalogue record for this book is available from the British Library.

10   9   8   7   6   5   4   3   2   1
21 20 19 18 17 16 15 14 13 12

Printed and bound in Great Britain by
the MPG Books Group, Bodmin and King's Lynn

To Janice, Linda, Kathleen, Maureen, David and Nancy
And our parents: Betty and Charlie
And Dave Mearns, one more brother

Contents

List of Boxes

List of Case Examples

Acknowledgements

Catherine Gray has been a gift of an editor, enhancing everything by her knowledge, judgement and love of writing. Dave Mearns and Ralph Keyes have been my best teachers of writing and John Keith Wood, much missed since his death, was my best teacher about the person-centred approach.

The following offered clinical insight and/or support of the writing process: Sandy Armstrong, Barb Bailey, Gay Swenson Barfield, Breffni Barrett, Gerald Boyd, Janice Campbell, Howard Campbell (much missed since his death), Lorna Carrick, Larry Chamow, Calvin Chou, Jamey Collins, Claire Comstock, Mick Cooper, Terry Daly, Bill Green, Jenni Johns, Molly Johns (beloved mother-in-law), Amina Knowlan, Elke Lambers, Brian Moriarty, Linda Moriarty, Elias Lefferman, Kathleen O'Leary Lefferman, Susan Lund, Jeanne McAlister, Christine McLean, Bob Mines, Jan Cooper Nadav (who deepened my connection to the work of Michael White), Jan Kerr, Maureen Ellen O'Leary, Barbara Reidell, Phil Rose, Morna Rutherford, David Sanders, Jim Thomas, Ron Urone, Eliot Weinstein, Astrid Whyte, Jan Wojcik, Doug and Marilyn Young, and Alberto Zuconni.

Carl Rogers contributed not only the richness of his legacy but the freshness his perspective brings to the work of therapists today. Emily Johns-O'Leary did a helpful tour of duty as an editor and offers lifelong encouragement as a daughter. Her sister Gwen is for me and many others a constant support and inspiration. My wife, Martha Johns, makes many things possible for me, including this book.

Foreword

I have known Charles O'Leary for forty years, back to a time when we were both attached to the Center for Studies of the Person (CSP) in La Jolla, California. The Resident Fellow of CSP was Dr Carl Rogers, then seventy years of age. Carl Rogers was very interested in the relationship of partners and had just published the book *Becoming Partners: Marriage and its Alternatives (1972)*. Charles O'Leary's fascination with the lives of couples and families mirrors that of his mentor, but his books do much more in actually helping practitioners to work as couple and family therapists. In that regard the present book goes much further than his earlier introductory text, *Counselling Couples and Families: A Person-Centred Approach (1999)* in its depth of analysis of the person-centred orientation as that applies to couple and family work. It also offers a more comprehensive review of theory and research from other family therapy traditions. The person-centred specialist, like therapists of any tradition, values a range of theory because that widens the therapist's imagination in the therapy room. For example, it would be inconceivable for a person-centred couple and family therapist to fail to have an appreciation of the systemic nature of family interaction. Similarly, a therapist whose primary influence is Systems Theory, would know that the sensitivity of therapeutic interventions is much increased if they are founded in the particular quality of empathy and valuing of the client that is fundamental for the person-centred practitioner.

An aspect of Charles O'Leary's work that is evident from this book is how *active* he is as a therapist. I found the same in work with couples, or even when I was working with a person who was actively representing different 'parts' of their self in conflict. Whenever we have more than one client in the room being 'client-centred' means that we have multiple responsibilities. Simultaneously we are responsible to the father who is dominating with his usual powerful voice, his wife who has been coping for years with this and the adolescent whose developed strategy has been to shut up and exert revenge by looking bored. The person-centred therapist has *all* these people as clients, simultaneously. Can the therapist show their empathy and their powerful valuing for each of them (including domineering characters) in the same moment? That takes an engaged and active therapist, probably also one who is able to use different 'parts' of themselves to engage with the range of experiences of their clients.

The shape of the book offers the reader regular sections where Charles O'Leary documents his 'thinking as a person-centred therapist' and also many case illustrations that have come to be a hallmark of his workshops and presentations in the USA and Europe.

Dave Mearns
Professor Emeritus, University of Strathclyde, Glasgow, Scotland
October, 2011

Introduction

A man and woman come to see me, estranged from their middle-aged only child because of some recent holiday scenes that brought almost 40 years of mutually frustrated desire for love and respect to the surface. I am an experienced family therapist and I think I know a great deal about how family life goes over time and have seen similar clients manage to make peace without denying integrity. I am also a person-centred therapist who knows nothing about each particular client in advance of meeting with and listening to them. My knowing, experienced professional self can offer questions, techniques, perspectives and a way forward; my receptive self can seek to understand and look for the questions, techniques, perspectives and way forward that may appear in the clients if they feel safe to be themselves with one another in my presence.

This book expresses my dialogue between the person-centred approach, in which I was first introduced to therapy in my first graduate programme, and the systems approach, in which I was schooled and supervised a few years later in my second graduate programme. I am always a couple and family therapist in dialogue with the person-centred approach and a person-centred therapist in dialogue with the many modalities of family therapy.

Research on therapy affirms that clients change for the better when four elements are in place:

- client motivation and response to events and developments in their lives;
- the quality of their relationship with the therapist;
- client hope that therapy will make a difference (placebo effect); and
- the specific model used by the therapist (Asay and Lambert 1999; Cooper 2008).

The core idea of all the chapters to follow is that a caring therapist who listens and who creates space for listening changes a system. I assert, in effect, that there are no valid techniques without connection. In work with families and couples bringing strong emotion and complex differing

1

needs, connection and help may only come through one of the many paths offered in the literature of systems therapy. Family therapy literature is, of course, journals, books, research studies and handbooks written by professionals for other professionals; it is also a true literature of stories and histories and narratives in which client voices are heard as well as the voices of therapists. Some 60 years of practice in this field that grew and developed contemporaneously with the person-centred approach have yielded a wealth of experience from caring men and women studying change in families. Similarly, the 70 years of person-centred literature reveal the stories of the unfolding of unique individual experiencing, facilitated by therapists open to their own inner life.

Relationship therapists are asked to meet each individual (especially child or teenager) on their own terms, while also understanding the worry, stress and even injury that person may cause others. A family therapist looks for clients to find their own way out of their troubles, while offering experience and knowledge that widen their perspective and reveal choices. A therapist must be powerful enough to set limits on mutual mistreatment, but client centred enough to make room for family ownership of the course of their lives. Couple therapists must make themselves ever more knowledgeable about the conditions in which attachment and respect can flourish, while being an attentive student of each couple's unique way of making their own relationship. Finally, the relationship therapist takes responsibility for facilitating an atmosphere of dialogue in each therapy hour, while having a beginner's mind, a learning attitude about the family's unique style and gifts. Insofar as the book is about me, it is about balancing my hard-won storehouse of ideas regarding how couples and families can get on with my curiosity about how these clients in front of me will find their way.

In 1957, a year after he was awarded one of the first two gold medals for scientific achievement by the American Psychological Association for his groundbreaking research on psychotherapy, Carl Rogers published an article entitled 'The necessary and sufficient conditions for therapeutic personality change' (1957). Famously, among those six conditions were: the need to understand the frame of reference of the client: the need for the therapist to be real; and the importance of an attitude of unconditional positive regard, also described as acceptance or prizing. Two of these conditions continue to be validated in contemporary couple and family therapy research and all six have continued to be the subject of study and research among person-centred and experiential therapists (Sprenkle et al. 2009). The way in which Rogers' conditions have shaped my work in the practice of therapy with couples and families is the subject of this book.

The book addresses concerns of an experienced therapist. How do you keep your work from becoming routine? It will offer many examples of therapist thinking and action that readers can use to reflect on their own unique responses to families and couples. My formulation of six attitudinal and behavioural practices in Chapter 2 provides a structure for a kind of dialogue faithful to couple and family therapy research that also takes advantage of the strengths of Carl Rogers' and his colleagues' 70 years of focus on the person of the therapist.

Although the person-centred approach was founded in the United States (Rogers 1980; Kirschenbaum and Henderson 1989), it is practised in a way most similar to its original style in the United Kingdom, Germany, Italy, Ireland, Japan and several other countries. Many university training programmes and curricula have focused on therapists' primary identities as facilitators and collaborators and have developed Carl Rogers' original insights and supportive research into a complex, humanistic theory and practice that challenge a medical model of human problems and solutions (Cooper et al. 2007). Though Carl Rogers remains the most influential psychotherapist in a recent survey of American practitioners (Simon 2007), the nature of his effect on the day-to-day work of thousands of relationship therapists is rarely articulated. In the world of family therapy over the last 20 years, an increasing emphasis on collaborative therapy (Madsen 2007), strengthening the clients' voices and individual empowerment articulated by post-modern therapy (Anderson 2001), dialogic therapy (Rober 2005) and narrative therapy (White 2007) has blended a client-centred perspective with systems awareness. This book will bring the voice of Carl Rogers and person-centred therapists into the conversation.

I am also writing this book to follow my first book, *Counselling Couples and Families: A Person-Centred Approach* (Sage, 1999), which was written primarily for therapists trained in individual therapy who follow the principles of the person-centred approach. That book offered an introduction for those familiar with the person-centred approach who were starting to see couples and families. It demonstrated a therapist's need to balance attention between each individual's unique process and awareness of their responsibility to be active in dialogue. This book goes further in describing the dialectic present for every effective couple therapist: How can differing perspectives co-exist in the same therapy? Besides being perceived as the ally of each person in the therapy, the therapist may live on both sides of the following dialectic:

The client is the individual	The client is the relationship between individuals
Feelings are the focus of attention	Ability to observe through a wider lens is the goal
Individual intention matters	Impact of words and actions matters equally
Focus on individual experience	Don't forget the importance of context
Differentiation is the goal	Connection and collaboration are the goals
Each speaks for themselves	Each individual expresses the whole field
Trust what you know inside	Let go of certainty: listen to outside information
Assert your needs and identity	Pay attention to others on their terms
You are unique	You exist and are co-created in dialogue
Be in the moment	Envision shared goals

While understanding and accepting each individual, the therapist must also manage to accept and understand the seemingly competing perspectives of their intimates. Each therapist may be also be asked to understand not only the current reality seen by the clients, but their preferred future realities and their lost, mourned-for past opportunities and expectations. Effective therapists manage to validate clients' description of their situation while remaining curious about other unspoken concerns and hopes as well as unnoticed resources.

Box 1: A Day with Carl Rogers and Virginia Satir

In 1979, Carl Rogers and family therapy founding mother Virginia Satir (Satir 1964, 1972) shared a stage at a day-long conference talking informally with one another and a large audience in an atmosphere of liking and respect for the other and the other's work. Each gave a talk; they shared a dialogue; each gave a demonstration of their work. Carl showed his intensely focused capacity to empathize with one client, to listen and show understanding of the world on the client's own terms. He stayed faithful as always to his practice of understanding what the client said on the client's terms, and his demonstration ended with the client feeling heard and understood. True to Rogers' frequently spoken conviction that what was most personal was also often most universal, the lesson for the audience was whatever they would gather from following one person's experience for 20 minutes.

Virginia showed her extraverted manner of empathic teaching in a demonstration with a family. She not only exemplified her caring ability to listen closely to and understand the people in front of her; she also transformed what they offered into a wide-ranging lesson about the family itself, family life in general and the way everyone in the audience might relate to one another. She asked frequent permission, sought client verification of what she was saying, but nonetheless transformed their words into a Virginia Satir experience.

The readers are invited to be aware of the style of both people in this book-length contemplation of couple and family therapy. Can they absorb the values of one person, quietly listening to each person who speaks, and of the other person, whose forceful personality gives permission for a whole system to risk change? None of us is the same as Carl Rogers or Virginia Satir. The clients that seek our help may look for qualities demonstrated by both in our practice of a person-centred couple and family therapy.

For therapists who are unfamiliar with or out of the habit of reflection on Carl Rogers' person-centred approach, I hope that this book is like meeting with a new consultant or temporary supervisor who may offer a new or renew a former perspective that can reawaken enthusiasm and respect for the practice of relationship therapy. Rogers still offers this service 23 years after his death. I can reread one of his books or articles or simply ask from memory: 'What would Rogers say if he saw this therapy hour or listened to what I thought about these clients?'

For readers from a person-centred background in individual or group therapy, the book offers a description of systems thinking, techniques and challenges. It builds on the essential skills described in my first book and offers ways to actively facilitate dialogue for distressed people while staying connected with individual feelings, perceptions and needs. The book offers the inspiration and techniques of several approaches to family and couple therapy that are compatible with a person-centred approach. Therapists may learn and borrow from many practitioners while using Rogers' core conditions as their compass. The book reflects on the tasks therapists face in early, middle and late therapy sessions. There is a full chapter on work with couples in general; another on work with gay and lesbian couples; and a third that describes work with families with children and teenagers. Each chapter offers case examples that illustrate a person-centred approach within a systems frame of reference.

I have never seen enough of what other therapists do when they meet with clients or heard enough about what they think about their clients and what they themselves should be doing. This book will attempt to show a person-centred approach as it exists in dozens of examples of therapy sessions. For some readers, some of these may offer ideas and a point of view that they can integrate into their own practice; others may find that my approach is different from their own and in that realization may have their own thinking validated and clarified.

Case Example 1: Systems Therapy and Nine Inch Nails

I once went to a concert by Nine Inch Nails. This is a rock group led by a man named Trent Reznor and is the kind of group that, no matter how old you are, your mother wouldn't let you go to, and certainly nothing a therapist over 50 should be allowed to see.

I had a 16-year-old client whom I didn't understand at all who loved Nine Inch Nails. I couldn't get what this group was about when he told me about them or when I listened to the CD I bought secondhand. I knew that this client was angry and lived in a condition of everyday bitterness, but I couldn't understand his delight in listening hour by hour to what seemed to me to be a celebration of hopelessness and ill-will. I could understand the reasons why my client's world was without trust, connection or consolation, but not why he seemed to choose it rather than look for passage out of it.

I was ignorant. I knew only two things: that perhaps someone should take a little trouble for him; and that I understood his mother much better than I did him.

So I bought a ticket for the concert. One ticket; nobody would go with me. A ticket worth more than an illegal campaign contribution bought a seat as far from the stage as you could be at Denver's Pepsi Center. My client implied, without explanation, that I might get hurt if I got any closer to the centre of action. He, of course, would be down in the really expensive place, the pit, where people banged into each other, lifted other kids up over their heads and, in general, did things to make each other pass out.

'Wear black,' he suggested firmly, happy to be in the role of adviser in the presence of his mother, 'so nobody notices you.' I stood in line with all these kids in leather and chains, with pierced bodies and chains coming out of pierced parts of their body and heavily made-up faces. I was wearing black, a T-shirt that has a skull on it and says 'Death Before Decaf'. My mobile phone was a lifeline. 'I'm going in,' I said to friends I called from the queue, as though crossing the border into Iraq. Going in came only after a search: I was thoroughly frisked with my hands held over my head by a young man who said, 'Thank you, sir.'

At the top of the Pepsi Center, a kid in the next seat fell into conversation with me and, after explaining why he was in such a pathetically cheap seat, became my guide for the evening. He was not surprised that I was a therapist there to try to understand dark music. (Apparently there are lots of therapists skulking around at these concerts.) 'We're here to go crazy. Get negative things out of our system. It's kind of like living out the Shadow for a while. This is not the way we really are.'

Nine Inch Nails is not the worst rock group in the world. The worst rock group in the world was the warm-up group before it. By the time Nine Inch Nails came along I was ready for relief – and I got it. The music was kind of Ok. Of course, I really couldn't understand the words. My friend in the next seat did a bit of translating, while lots of kids sang along to their old familiar favourites about self-destruction and general loathing. We were all standing up and, after a while, even I was dancing to the music, there in the dark in the last row. When the kids reverently held up lighters, I believe I lit a wooden match. It felt a bit like being at Woodstock, if only my mother had allowed me to go to it.

I had gone to the Pepsi Center to learn and left understanding not Nine Inch Nails exactly, or at all, but why my client might love them. He needed to feel what he felt, surrounded by other people feeling what he felt, listening to someone who said what he felt, before he could have any freedom to move on. Nine Inch Nails was not his destination, I hoped, but was necessary for his journey. I speculated on this while realizing that I am incredibly out of it.

Nevertheless, things were different between us. I had done something out of a wish to change a relationship for the better and even if I didn't understand, I had shown that I wanted to. It changed nothing in terms of my control over how this person thought or acted, but I had shortened the distance between us by my efforts. Empathy is like that: it is the willingness to understand at least as much as the talent to do so. Genuine empathy in your relationships, especially with an intimate adversary, may well make you feel as strange as a therapist, away from his books, listening to Trent Reznor.

'You went?' my client said, surprised. 'Cool.'

1

The Challenges of Person-Centred Relationship Therapy

Having lived among family and couple therapists for many years, I will present some of their ideas and techniques that I find compatible with the six conditions of effective therapy outlined elegantly by Carl Rogers over 60 years ago. In this chapter and Chapter 2, I will offer a personal tour of my approach to couple and family therapy, briefly discussing therapists whose post-modern approaches to families, including narrative therapy, share core person-centred values.

In this chapter, I will also present what clients say are their goals in relationship therapy and discuss three challenges for all couple and family therapists that lend themselves to a person-centred approach:

- multi-directional partiality;
- use of relationship knowledge and skills;
- and active facilitation.

I offer reflections on the specific qualities of a person-centred approach, including the first presentation of Rogers' core conditions for therapy. A final case example shows a therapist at work, integrating a person-centred approach with a family therapy perspective.

The World of the Relationship Therapist

Relationship therapists always work in between co-existing, different realities. In practice, a therapist cannot get completely absorbed in tracking an individual's process without attention to the reactions of others in the room. Similarly, any description of a group condition must co-exist with awareness of its effect on each individual's perceptions and self-concept. The therapist never stops being a translator looking for points of understanding among very different internal countries.

Research shows that the therapist/client relationship does not only depend on therapist qualities such as empathy and acceptance; it is also important that clients see therapists as aligned with their spoken and unspoken goals (Sprenkle et al. 2009). Couples come to therapists because they cannot talk to one another without inhibition, discouragement or real or feared rejection. Families come either because something seems to have gone wrong with one or more children, or because the children's progress from one stage to another has caused emotional unbalance involving fear, anger, disconnection or discouragement. Every therapist must not stray far from each client's expressed or implicit goal, both as they state it in the beginning and as it evolves.

What Do Clients Want?

Here are some goals that I commonly discover with my clients:

- To be able to be their authentic self without losing the love and approval of their loved ones.
- To solve a problem or to return to a better level of cooperation in the face of a complex predicament.
- To be able to talk cooperatively with one another about 'the great thing in the middle of the room' (Palmer 1997), whether it be sex, money, parents, child development, dreams, disappointments, transitions, individual growth, grief or the loss of 'the way we used to be'.
- To have their shortcomings overlooked, accepted or at least not to be the subject of scolding and shaming.
- To have their strengths remembered and noted at least as much as their failings.
- To be respected: not to be yelled at but also not to be ignored.
- To be able to back away and be left alone when they want to be.
- To be noticed for their own sake rather than as a subject of someone else's expectations.
- To express their ideas of what is fair and appropriate.
- To be given a second chance if they have made a mistake, misbehaved or otherwise disappointed a significant other.
- To have their reasons for acting in a way that displeases their loved ones at least acknowledged, occasionally understood and even sometimes validated.

- To be able to manage family cohesion while the drama of growth pushes towards separation.
- To acknowledge losses, impasses and disappointments without resorting to blame, rejection, threats and rigid categorization.
- To be able to adjust to ever-changing boundaries, authority, availability and norms of mutual respect.
- To have a way to carry all these experiences out of the therapy office into their day-to-day lives.

There are also goals specific to couple therapy (see especially Greenberg and Goldman 2008a, b; or Moser and Johnson 2008):

- To resolve problems of closeness: more affection, more security in attachment.
- To be able to return to moments of perceived mutual or individual injury and begin the process of repair without repeating the injury.
- To resolve problems of power, significance, respect, autonomy and identity in a relationship context.
- To identify, resolve or learn to live with pressures from children, ex-partners, families of origin and friends.
- To restore friendship.
- To stop fighting and to stop avoiding talking about significant issues.

The World of One Relationship Therapist

What does couple and family therapy mean to me in the hours in which I practise it? Having been introduced to therapy from the person-centred approach, I am a listener who does not intend to judge or control. I also have a hundred ideas in the back of my mind, derived from 35 years of systems therapy-related reading, training and practice. All those perspectives are part of me: not external techniques I laboriously drag out, but possibilities that naturally emerge in meetings with clients. Below are nine ideas, from diverse therapy traditions, that are my constant companions and will be illustrated throughout this book. I offer them as a description of my own integration of theory and practice rather than as a prescription for the reader. Each family and couple therapist can seek their own path to useful, caring relationship facilitation.

1. *The dynamic of the core conditions of the person-centred approach* (Rogers 1957; O'Leary 1999, 2008; Gaylin 2001, 2008). Described in detail

below and especially in Chapter 4, the interaction of empathy, acceptance and realness is the beginning and end of my work. I meet with people and join them in invariably confusing circumstances and competing beliefs. My core centring, always useful, intervention is to stop and listen and seek to understand from clients in a non-judgemental way. There is no systems intervention more essential. All the perspectives listed below enhance the clients' experience of these conditions or are not helpful.

2. *Reframing.* The heart of all systems therapy (Framo 1996), changing the core description of an interpersonal predicament or problem in such a way that wider lens perceptions are allowed, dialogue is encouraged and positive possibilities can emerge. Family therapist and teacher Jim Thomas says, 'In family work, it's a different take: unconditional positive regard requires reframing' (personal communication). Family therapy models, writes one theorist (Beels 2009), 'when stripped of their theoretical dressing are ways of focusing a common agreement in a room where two or more people feel passionate disagreement about the meaning of the experience'. The listening therapist seeks to translate raw interpersonal distress into a predicament that can be discussed with less blame, fear and provocation. Almost all the therapist's statements have qualities of reframing. Person-centred empathy reframes client words simply by the transformation of something said tentatively, passionately or even provocatively into something that is heard respectfully and taken seriously without judgement, defensiveness or drama. Relationship therapists listen closely, finding within impossible (accusatory or hopeless) conversations the core needs and wishes that drive them. The art of therapy is to provide fresh language without suppressing urgent feelings.

3. *Dominant story/alternate story.* This concept from narrative therapy (White and Epston 1990) allows whatever distress clients express to be retold as part of a story that has emerged in their lives rather than as a symptom of intrinsic inadequacy on their part. This therapist always looks for a narrative that describes a whole experience in a way that includes all participants. The concept of the dominant story is a most imaginative form of systems thinking: people are seen as living in a virtual, prescribed dramatic scenario in which their choices and experiences are limited and disabling. Naming a story and inviting clients to comment on or add to it allows the opportunity for the clients to remember their own ability to choose their responses in the face of that story. The therapist holds an active

curiosity about what alternative, overlooked, more encouraging story may co-exist and offer resources to clients. Here is the story that I am hearing so far,' a therapist might say. Later that therapist might say, 'I am meeting two people who are living in a sad house. Your marriage has become this place of "never saying or doing the right thing" rather than the new land of closeness and pride you expected it to be. Do I have this right?'

4. *Taking the 'I' position.* This concept, from family therapy founding father Murray Bowen (1978), represents a way of being in one's family of origin and exactly parallels the intentions of a congruent person-centred therapist. Therapists speak their own truth without attempting to impose that truth on another. The direct sharing of a therapist speaking from within a situation *without an agenda for others or judgement of them* is central to clients' experience of an opportunity either to accept themselves and others or to initiate change. The therapist is a person first and a therapist or expert second. Claiming the freedom to speak for oneself in a respectful way invites clients into a calmer form of conversation, in which they don't have always to be right or even on someone else's point in order to be heard.

5. *Externalizing the problem.* This is the core expression in narrative therapy of an old therapeutic tool found in Jungian psychology, psychodrama and Gestalt therapy: finding a way to *personify* common sources of distress for all members of a couple or family rather than locating trouble in the persons within the group (Freedman and Combs 1996). For example: 'The Land of the Perpetual Fight'; 'Nagging mother/frustrating teen'; 'The "can't-do-anything-right family"'. Each phrase is helpful only if it allows clients to see themselves as caught in a pattern rather than as personally in the wrong. I may frequently say, 'The *American (or British, or Italian etc.) idea of marriage* is out to get this couple.' This last is a favourite of mine: almost invariably, clients are discouraged by the difference between their own relationship and an idealized relationship that they feel they *are supposed to be having.*

6. *Asking reflection-oriented questions.* This invokes client curiosity and the possibility of creating a different process. Influenced by the 'circular questions' of the Milan group (Boscolo et al. 1987) as well as the questions developed by solution-oriented practitioners (de Shazer 1982, 1994; Berg and Miller, 1992), therapists make enquiries that allow unspoken hopes, fears, memories, disappointments and possibilities to emerge. For example: 'What were things like when

you all did get along, even back in the 1940s?' 'Who in your life do you think would be most convinced that you can solve this problem?' 'What would your best friend wish we were talking about?' 'How do you think your parents would react if they were in the same situation are you are?' When clients have managed something they had thought impossible, I may ask: 'What do you think may now be possible for you, now that you have ("finished high school", "got this job", "managed a weekend in which you didn't fight even once).'

7. *Holding and expressing awareness of human development and consequent change in roles, boundaries and hierarchy.* These core ideas of structural family therapy (Minuchin 1974; Mitriani and Perez 2003) help make family distress more understandable than the blame–disappointment orientation that can emerge in an individual's perspective. Every person changes with time and thereby affects the self-concept of every other person in their life. The role and security of a parent may be threatened by the greater autonomy of a child; a woman's great sense of her own needs and rights may be a threat to both her partner, her children and other family-of-origin members. This awareness can normalize (allow events to be seen as natural and predictable) troubles that otherwise would be considered signs of inadequacy or bad intentions.

8. *Spatial arrangement, movement and other choreography.* Family therapy founding mother Virginia Satir used every inch of space in whatever setting to allow clients literally new perspectives (Satir 1972; Papp 1983). As a way of responding to many seemingly opposed descriptions of trouble, I frequently stand up and walk around to locate different aspects of the situation in different parts of the room. I may invite a couple to move to two different chairs so that they can leave the 'fight' back where they were sitting. Using movement on the part of clients as well as the therapist is especially important when children are part of the group. More important than any single action is the knowledge that I, the therapist, don't have to sit in the place of distress but can move about in search of non-distressed possibilities.

9. *Enactments* (Mitrani and Perez 2003; Butler et al. 2008; Moser and Johnson 2008). Clients can be frustrated by the difference between their less anxious, more civil behaviour in therapy and their frustrating interactions at home. In enactments, clients replicate a form of their conflict at home in the office where:

    - each person, including the therapist, can stop the action and report on what they are feeling;

- each person can share observations about what the conflict means and what alternatives to it could look like;
- the clients could try out other ways of expressing or responding that would give the interaction a different meaning or outcome.

Enactments can bring clients' worst experiences into a climate in which empathy, realness and acceptance allow changes in perspective and in behaviour.

A person-centred couple and family therapist, as jazz musician Wynton Marsalis says, responds to what other players in the room offer; they contribute their own sound but don't impose something that doesn't connect with what is already there. The purpose of the perspectives and tools described above and any other techniques is to provide resources that facilitate conversation in which clients feel heard, safe to be themselves, empowered and respected. An experienced systems therapist may ask themselves what are their own core attitudes and techniques and why. My own attempts to find a way of conversation that joins with my clients' own voices parallels the work of the therapists briefly described in Box 1.1.

Box 1.1: Collaborative, Post-modern and Dialogic Therapies

Post-modernism is a term that is applied to such therapists as Harlene Anderson, Lynn Hoffman and Peter Rober, all of whom are part of my internal chorus of encouragers as a relationship therapist. Post-modern 'refers to a family of concepts that have developed among scholars … that call for an ideological critique – a questioning perspective – of the relevance and consequences of foundational knowledge, metanarratives and privileged discourses, including their certainty and power for our everyday lives' (Anderson 1997).

Though *Harlene Anderson* describes her writing as a 'philosophy of therapy' rather than a theory, her use of language has practical consequences: *no one* defines a person or their difficulties from outside; the nature of problems changes through family interaction characterized by listening and respect. These ideas have urgency, for example in therapy with minorities such as gay and lesbian couples, discussed in Chapter 6. In practice, Harlene Anderson sees therapy as a conversation among equals in which each member of a family has their own story about what their family is. Listening to each story allows language to be 'relational and generative' and brings about a new, co-constructed reality for clients that can be 'transformational'. Comparing herself with Carl Rogers, Anderson (2001) identifies with his client-centredness and rejection of diagnosis and other positions that make the therapist expert and in control. She distinguishes herself from him in being a more active conversational partner and being more 'public', sharing more of her own voice in the therapy. Famously, with her colleague the late Harry Goolishian she has written about the 'not knowing position' (a term used also by person-centred therapist Peter Schmid 2002, 2004), which refers not, of course, to therapist's lack of knowledge but to openness to learning from the clients' own words and presentation (Goolishian and Anderson 1992). The therapist comes to each meeting without 'prior knowledge' about what the clients' situation and feelings might be and seeks to understand what the client understands without translating it into the language of the expert helper.

Lynn Hoffman is a family therapy elder whose biography associates her closely with the earliest family therapy theorists, such as Jay Haley, Virginia Satir, anthropologist Gregory Bateson, Salvador Minuchin and, especially in later years, Harlene Anderson, Harry Goolishian and other post-modernists, as well as narrative therapist Michael White. See her *Family Therapy: An Intimate History* (2002) for her rich life finding her own voice among all these originals. Hoffman offers a personalized and free exploration and integration of all family therapy ideas and encourages practitioners to expose clients to those ideas without imposing them as an expert. In support of each meeting with clients as a unique experience, she encouraged 'Setting aside the model' (1998), any model that makes the therapist the holder of privileged truth. Hoffman (2002) offers many conditions for her integrated, centred-on-persons approach to therapy, including the following:

- 'Embracement', which is a form of acceptance that is open to all clients as well as their whole situation.
- 'Tempathy' or 'traveling empathy', which refers to therapists' openness to their own voices meeting with client voices and the sharing of images that emerge for client reflections. Hoffman encourages reflective involvement in client situations, with the results of therapist intuition made available for client use.
- 'Generous listening' – that is, not 'listening in order to speak' but 'speaking in order to listen'.
- 'Knowledge of the third kind'. This term from John Shotter (1993) refers not to theoretical knowledge (knowing that) or even practical knowledge (knowing how), but knowledge that comes from being within a situation – knowing from lived experience. The therapist brings their experience, knowledge and professional training into a meeting about which they cannot know and of which they do not control the outcome. What they do contribute is readiness to response to what is present. Although they have many thoughts and skills, they offer what is called for in the interaction rather than anything they can prepare. They bring a way of being to the therapy that is instinctual as well as cognitive; personal as well as professional.

Peter Rober is a Belgian psychologist who also looks to 'knowing of the third kind' to describe his approach to 'dialogic family therapy' (2005). Rober quotes Shotter (1993: 40–41) regarding knowledge 'in terms of which people are able to influence each other in their being, rather than just in their intellects: that is, to actually "move" them rather than just giving them ideas'. Exploring dialogue in a series of articles (1999, 2002, 2005, 2008) that capture the 'therapist's inner conversation' (2008) as well as the many levels in which clients' words may be understood, Rober describes a therapy of respectful presence in which therapists listen to clients' voices and their own voices simultaneously. Regarding family therapy, he reminds us that dialogue is continuous and that every therapy session enters an ongoing dialogue that preceded the session and will continue after it.

I am at home in the world of post-modernists, but I do not identify specifically with their or any philosophical approach. This book describes therapy steeped in Carl Rogers' clarifying basic principles that allow client autonomy and growth within a systems perspective. Like Hoffman, I feel free to borrow generously from therapies that preceded post-modernism without complete allegiance to their theories. All authors about relationship therapy have in common thousands of hours in the presence of families or couples: their activity, their decisions not to act, their way of configuring family distress and family resources.

The Purpose of Relationship Therapy

Relationship therapy facilitates the, sometimes elusive, process of being a differentiated person – a separate 'I' – who must make autonomous decisions and live with complicated feelings while remaining part of an intimate group capable of mutual support, understanding and apprecia-tion. In her hundreds of public demonstrations, family therapy founding mother Virginia Satir used to connect all family members with ropes and encourage them to move about. She thus illustrated that one person's motion necessarily exerts a pull on every other person. Each movement of other people pulls the original person. (See Chapter 3 for a more detailed discussion of systems thinking.) Family or couple therapy becomes necessary when clients are, so to speak, pulling one another in opposite directions, or when one or more people are paralysed for fear of pulling or being pulled too hard or in the wrong direction.

The purpose of family therapy, says Peter Rober (2005), is to find 'a way to get on'. Harlene Anderson says that it is to have 'problems not solved but dis-solved' (1997). She means that changing the nature of *conversations* changes what couples and families face (1997: 108–31). When couples and families come to see me it is because they cannot talk with each other about their real needs and troubles, and instead must choose between blaming, fighting and avoiding talk of what is most important. A therapist facilitates a way to bring troubling topics into a room without driving people out. Family therapy offers clients a way to grow in each other's presence rather than privately struggling with discouragement and frustration. Relationship therapy facilitates individual discovery with respect for its impact on family connectedness. A good relationship therapist facilitates discovery of unseen family group patterns, with attention to the implications for individual self-concept. The therapist also looks for unexpected, understated changes in individual self-concept that may open doors for system-wide change.

Contemporary couple and family therapists have many issues to resolve for which a person-centred approach may be helpful. They must be engaged without being reactive; confident and knowledgeable without being superior or controlling. They must avoid getting trapped in 'impossible therapy' by feelings of urgency, anxiety, over-responsibility or pessimism, in Duncan, Hubble and Miller's brilliant formulation (1997a). Relationship therapy brings, among others, three challenges: the need for multi-directional partiality, a knowledge of the conditions and common patterns of couple and family life, and the need for active facilitation of change that is compatible with each client's sense of self-respect and of timing. I now look at each of these important ideas in turn.

- *Multi-directional partiality.* This is crucial to relationship therapy and is the intention and practice of being on everyone's side at the same time (Boszormenyi-Nagy et al. 1991; O'Leary 1999). In person-centred terms it is about contact/empathy of equal quality with everyone in the room. See Chapter 2 for a fuller discussion of this topic. The relationship therapist facilitates a meeting between different people who may be caught in complex habits and troubled by years of not feeling understood by one another. Person-centred therapy begins and ends with attention to each person's unique perspective, while clarifying and validating other perspectives in the same room. The therapist models the expectation that contradictory interests must co-exist in order to allow conversation to take place. Most people, however good their intentions, have at least some negative impact on those they love most. Finding room for understanding the reality of negative impacts without denying good intentions requires a person-centred connection with both perceived victims and perceived offenders. It also takes the skill and personal authority to facilitate dialogue when hurt feelings are activated. For example, the therapist is understanding both of the young person who makes black-and-white pronouncements about his parents' failings and of the mother or father struggling to find their new place in their child's life. The therapist, managing internal comfort with the fact that two things can be true at the same time, seeks to be a believable translator between seemingly irreconcilable inner realities.

- *Knowledge of the conditions and common patterns of couple and family life.* A person-centred therapist privileges clients' own knowledge and ability to solve problems while consciously committing to know as much as possible about 'how life is lived between sessions' (Barrett-Lennard 2005). Clients need a therapist to be knowledgeable about life in a couple or family and to have skills that clients can use.

  Therapists cannot know everything and, wisely, never forget how much they do not know. At the same time, the more a therapist learns about contemporary relationship expectations, the more clients can feel that they are in the presence of someone who understands what their life is like. Knowledge can lead to deeper and more accurate empathy, while making the therapist a reliable collaborator in problem solving. Similarly, most clients eventually ask for skills to use when they are at home: the therapist may offer tools for communication, problem solving, a genogram (a type of family tree used in intergenerational therapies, to be described in detail in Chapter 3), printed guidelines, books and CDs that relate to the problems that the clients identify.

  Lynn Hoffman has written (1998: 153): 'I have proposed a category called Biggest Hits of Family Therapy. Our field is full of wondrous things that we can use even if we do not accept the theories that produced them.'

- *Active facilitation of change.* Couples and families come to therapy for the resolution of problems and the unravelling of predicaments. A therapist must be an active facilitator who makes dialogue possible – someone who can 'discuss all undiscussable issues' (Schwartz 2002) and who also seeks to give a voice to all present and to acknowledge the effects on each person's feelings. The therapist is listener, supporter and moderator, timekeeper and respectful process director. The therapist is in the sorting out business: seeing what issues belong to whom, which can be solved immediately and which must be understood better before being addressed, which are signs of an untenable understanding and which are just part of life. The good therapist encourages clients to find a description of a situation that encourages dialogue, deflects the tendency to blame and engenders human-sized hope. Finally, the therapist facilitates the necessary movement between acting for change and accepting lack of readiness to change.

Narrative therapy, briefly described in Box 1.2, provides perspectives and language that facilitate clients' empowerment by discovering their identity that is separate from their problems, circumstances and definitions by others.

Box 1.2: Narrative Therapy – Problem-Saturated Stories and Unique Outcomes

Narrative therapy is work originated by the late Michael White and David Epston, famously described in their classic *Narrative Means to Therapeutic Ends* (1990), in Freedman and Combs' *Narrative Therapy: The Social Construction of Preferred Realities* (1996) and most recently in Michael White's last book (2007), *Maps of Narrative Practice*. Narrative therapy sees clients as 'trapped in problem-saturated stories' in which attempts to solve the problem often increase the power of the problem. In their post-modernist frame of reference, White and Epston see clients as identified with their problems by the social definitions of their immediate community as well as, in many ways, by the larger culture. Therapy consists, therefore, in changing the conversation in such a way that the client is seen as separate from the problem that distresses them and competent to reduce its influence. This is a therapy in which language is challenged as a potential means of oppression.

White famously asks questions that involve clients becoming 'investigative reporters' (2007) into their problems: how they have affected them; how they might be defeated; what plans the problems have for ruining their lives; and what strengths they and their other family members might have for getting them out of their lives. His questions exist 'to generate experience rather than gather information' (Freedman and Combs 1996: 113). His questions generate metaphors through which clients take positions towards changing the problems in their lives.

Narrative therapy engages imagination, wonder and especially, like the person-centred approach, the assumption that people have untapped resources that flourish when they are outside categories dominated by fear, blame or judgement. David Epston once said, 'we must forever be realizing that people are multi-storied, just as our stories of culture and psychology are. For instance, what would have happened if Carl Rogers' work had been the privileged psychological text rather than Freud's? It would seem that we would have a totally different psychological world' (quoted in Madigan 1994). In the world of narrative therapy as well as the person-centred approach, there is the way people are when diminished by what Rogers calls the 'evaluative tendency' (1961), similar to what White calls the 'dominant story' (1990). There is also the experience of freedom 'to be the self one truly is' (Rogers 1961) and the 'intentional self' (White 2007) when people are freed from external control and evaluation.

Narrative therapy offers a rich language for finding the effects of the actualizing tendency, a core concept of the person-centred approach, described below (Rogers 1980, 1959). The opposite of the problem-saturated story is the appearance of unique outcomes; that is, experiences in which a problem was expected to occur but did not because of effort or imagination by clients. The concept of unique outcomes focuses clients' attention on their resources, their unnoticed good habits and good practices and, in couples and families, on what they are like when they are not trapped in the story called 'fight about everything' or 'we can't get along any more'. I frequently send clients home with a small notebook and the request that they make note of such things as: 'When you would usually be scheduled to fight but didn't' or 'When (your partner) would usually disappoint you but didn't.' White encourages client and therapist to investigate each unique outcome with questions such as: 'What is it that made it possible for you to listen rather than defend yourself?' 'What does it say about your relationship that after all you have been through you were able to make love that night?' 'What might be possible between you now that you know that you can get through a conflict and still be not only speaking to one another but each feeling like you are with a friend.'

Narrative approaches give room for the presence of understanding and compassion in a relationship field that is often swamped by negativity, fuelled by fear of rejection and unfairness. It allows for giving validity to the unspoken hope of closeness that does not deny frustration, grief and hurt. A couple and family therapist needs language in which to create a context for new events and reclaiming of old, supportive events that have been forgotten or buried by understanding and disappointment. The therapist can remain client-centred while creating space for couple and family members to take responsibility for attempting to understand as well as seeking to be understood.

Core Values in the Person-Centred Approach

What kind of person is the therapist, regardless of the particular model they use? David Bott has commented regarding family therapy:

> Pragmatically, if we are seeking to humanize our practice and respond respectfully to families with a view to creating a context which empowers rather than subjugates, Rogers provides a clear, accessible and, above all, ethical position from which to do this. (Bott 2001: 375)

The starting points for understanding the person-centred approach are Rogers' six necessary and sufficient conditions for helpful therapeutic meeting (1957), described below as applied to relationship therapy. Mearns and Thorne (2000) have described the six conditions as interactive, each inseparable from the others. Furthermore, they describe these conditions in terms of 'becoming ready to meet the other' (2000: 87–100). Each therapist, skilled and knowledgeable as they seek to be, is always engaged in becoming a person whom clients will find trustworthy, affirming and encouraging. Without work on ourselves, we face the possibility of being the opposite. Rogers found that his six conditions allowed individuals to emerge from a pattern of blocked development. Family systems therapy in its myriad forms has had a similar goal.

Here is the first statement of these conditions applied to couple and family therapy:

1. *Psychological contact with each client.* The consistent intent to connect with each person present in every session facilitates change in the system of several persons.
2. *Awareness of a state of incongruence causing anxiety in both individual and system.* A person-centred therapist expects, accepts and works with incongruence: mixed messages, contradictory feelings, inconsistent or even deceitful behaviour. The therapist relates not with judgement but by attention to understand all and to acknowledge more congruent aspects of person and relationship.
3. *Therapist congruence (authenticity or integrity).* In order to be trusted for dialogue about clients' most treasured relationships, the therapist must be personally integrated so that their words match their actions and their affect. Only a real person can be trusted with the deepest experiences of important relationships.
4. *Therapist unconditional positive regard.* Families and couples can become open and confident enough for change only if therapists are perceived as *accepting each person as they are rather than judging.*
5. *Therapist empathy.* Each person feels the therapist's intention to understand their internal frame of reference – in relationship therapy, also to understand the shared predicament between persons.
6. *Clients perceive the above conditions.* Therapists share in whatever way will allow clients to experience therapist, realness, acceptance and empathy.

The person-centred approach is an outlook, a set of priorities and the result of a series of commitments. For every therapist, in every session, there is the path of the expert in control or the path of the collaborator, who is always centred on the experience of the clients. The person-centred therapist is biased towards client unfolding rather than fitting the client into any predetermined pattern. Such a therapist ' "(speaks) in order to listen" as opposed to "listening in order to speak" ', as family therapy historian Lynn Hoffman (2002: 181) said about Carl Rogers. The therapist supports client control; is alert for overlooked potential; and seeks the free expression of clients' experience of truth without setting off judgemental assumptions.

Person-centred therapists also are committed to lifelong self-aware-ness and development. They seek to be non-defensive about their own limitations, even while they are open to the discovery of clients' undis-covered possibilities. Person-centred supervision focuses as much on the therapist's state of mind as on the client's (Lambers 2006). John Keith Wood (2008) described Carl Rogers in several settings, then observed:

> Although his apparent reaction, his manner of expression, his feelings and circumstances may have been different in each of these situa-tions, I believe Rogers *approached* them in the very same way. He approached each situation with the same desire to understand, the same good humor, the same humility, the same honesty, the same non-judgmental acceptance of the individual or the group, the same curiosity and openness to learning, the same will to facilitate a constructive outcome for the individual or group. He improvised from his knowledge and abilities in each specific case. (2008: 20)

As a person-centred couple and family therapist, there is always more than one voice in my head. Like Peter Rober (2008), I am my experienc-ing self, with my own emotional and intellectual reactions, meeting with other people; as well as my professional self, responsible for choices based on my training and the expectations of the clients. I am always in a brand new, never-before-known meeting with clients and am, as well, the carrier of the practical, theoretical and research findings of systems therapy. The person-centred approach has been described in many of Rogers' works (particularly 1961, 1980; Kirschenbaum and Henderson 1989, 1990) and interpreted and expanded in the work of Mearns and Thorne (2000, 2007), Barrett-Lennard (1998) and most recently Cooper et al. (2007, forthcoming). Here are four elements of the person-centred approach that I carry with me:

- *Self-concept and the ideal self.* Therapists are sensitive to the differ-ence between self-concept, a picture of self that clients experi-ence and evaluate, and ideal self, a picture of self living up to the expectations of self and others, as it shows itself in fear, doubt and frustration in individuals as well as the whole group. Person-centred empathy facilitates clients' awareness of expectations that drain confidence and fuel frustration. One outcome of relationship ther-apy may be a client saying something like: 'If I focus on who we are,

I relax; if I think about the marriage I expected to have, I get tense.' The self-concept of each individual attracts therapist attention and care, even while they attempt to understand and facilitate dialogue about interpersonal concerns and possibility. The congruence between self-concept and ideal self in any individual at any age affects the self-concept of the entire family. In couple and family therapy, clients often see a change in a loved one's self-concept as a threat to their own. In a couple, when one person becomes more independent it can seem that the other is less important. In a family, a new close relationship can make it seem that a child or a parent is no longer important. Chapter 3 on systems thinking will discuss the seesaw-like effect of change among intimates.

- *Clients experience themselves as in charge of the therapy.* The therapist may offer suggestions, structures, comments and perspective, but only what has resonance or meaning for the clients is a lasting focus. Rogers described the locus (place) of evaluation that resides in the client rather than the therapist (1959). This concept is similar to the Bowen systems idea of differentiation (Friedman 1991). It refers to the ability of clients to separate their own feelings and intentions from those they have absorbed from others. The more the clients feel that their own judgements are attended to and trusted, the more they take effective control of their own lives. A person-centred approach encourages a higher trust in clients' own perspective and a lessening of attention to 'shoulds' imposed from outside. In a summary of years of research about clients' experience of therapy, John McLeod (2006) asserted: 'Clients consider themselves the producers of their own treatment.' They also 'have countless more thoughts than they tell their therapists'. Being client-centred is not the absence of therapist power; it is the presence of attention to client power. A person-centred relationship therapist facilitates clients' ability to talk about differences without having to blame or reject.
- *Actualizing tendency.* Therapeutic practice revolves around the concept of the 'actualizing tendency' or 'innate capacity for human beings to move toward fulfillment of their potential' (Mearns and Thorne 1988). The perception that all clients' words and actions are, in some way, clients' attempts to become their fullest selves can be a powerful ally in sorting out couples and families in distress. Listening, attempting to understand and attempting to make sense out of seemingly impossible predicaments all derive power from the integration of this core concept. Person-centred supervision – actually, any helpful

supervision I have ever had – finds its centre in the trust of that in clients that is trying to survive and grow. This core principle of the person-centred approach is compatible with the family therapy tradition of reframing, 'offering a different perspective which changes the meaning of an event or process (usually but not always in more positive terms)' (O'Leary 1999: 36) and 'emphasis on the positive' (Hoffman 1998). Without neglecting the expectation that problems will be addressed if not resolved, person-centred therapists prioritize finding the family's best intentions rather than fixing their perceived deficiencies.

- *Evaluative tendency.* Therapists hold the belief that 'the evaluative tendency', judgements of others' actions and words, causes many if not most human relationship problems (Rogers 1961). In this, they may parallel narrative therapists, who seek to redefine relationship troubles as processes that oppress all involved rather than the product of one person's bad intentions or lack of competence. The therapist can never do away with the tendency to judge, but can listen for alternative ways of understanding that which is judged. Clients, of course, bring many judgements of one another into every session. The therapist does not argue with or blame clients for these judgements, but focuses on the wishes and intentions behind them. At best, all clients find themselves in an 'error-friendly zone' (Lambers 2006). Their efforts and intentions are more important than their perceived shortcomings. The work of empathy is, in part, about making room for co-existing good intentions in the presence of complicated predicaments. Therapists accept clients exactly as they are in the situation they are in and facilitate that acceptance in client relationships. Insofar as a person becomes expert in the person-centred approach, they develop a facility, not of showing clients what is right but in relating so that clients feel less in the wrong.

Case Example 1.1: Family Therapy Walks in the Door

This case illustrates the practice of multi-directional partiality, knowledge of the way developmental change appears in the form of trouble and active facilitation through a crisis to higher level of organization. I will also show the importance of readiness to see how development (e.g. a child becoming an almost-adult) changes a system's functioning in ways that produce strong emotions. The case also illustrates a simple kind of choreography that allows people to have strong feelings without victimizing a loved one.

Peter was not, as scheduled, in the waiting room alone: he was accompanied by his wife, Linda, and their 15-year-old son, Josh. Linda and Josh, sitting as far away from Peter as the physics of the room allowed, looked as grim as Peter looked angry. Linda had insisted that all come in for Peter's appointment because of a scene between Peter and Josh just before it was time to leave for my office. Peter had lashed out at his son, who, because of a painfully intrusive disorder, with physical as well as psychological symptoms, has usually been treated with loving, permissive, almost unlimited attention.

In my office, with Peter glaring at her and Josh sitting close to her, Linda began to talk.

LINDA: I heard Peter saying terrible things to Josh and I said, 'We've got to resolve this tonight. We're all going in to see Charles.'

THERAPIST: It's an emergency. We've got to bring this into the therapy. Something has to stop. *(The therapist empathizes with the individual. Claiming the right to do that, in itself, slows down the family process.)*

LINDA: Exactly. I mean, Josh isn't perfect but Peter's supposed to be the grown-up and what kind of example is he setting with the things he said?

THERAPIST: So, Peter, you agreed to have Linda and Josh come with you although all of you are angry and upset. *(The therapist continues to slow down the process and explicitly reflects a shared state of mind as well as purposeful action in the face of angry conflict.)*

PETER (with some bitterness): I didn't have much choice, but this is fine. It all needs to come out. We're both supposed to bend over backwards for him [Josh] but we are never supposed to ask anything of him. Well, it's got to stop!

THERAPIST: You're so frustrated right now. It's as though you've got to change everything about how the family does things. You want it known that Josh and Linda can't expect so much of you. *(The therapist both empathizes with Peter's feelings as well as acknowledging the possibility of an important communication about change in the midst of a seemingly directionless fight.)*

PETER: I've had it. (To Josh) You don't do a damn thing to help yourself. So we have to treat you with kid gloves!

THERAPIST: *(drawing the angry force away from Josh)* You are really feeling it's not fair. You feel overwhelmed about what Josh seems to expect of you.

PETER: Well, it's all got to change. *We* have to be perfect. He can have and do anything he wants!

The therapist is drawing on the concept of choreography brought into family therapy from psychodrama by Virginia Satir and Peggy Papp, among others (Papp 1983). The therapist allows Peter to speak angrily to him about feelings, while the original object of the feelings can observe them rather than take their emotional force directly. Peter's (or any person's) need to vent does not mean another family member has to absorb his angry energy.

The therapist continues to reflect Peter's expressions as feelings Peter has rather than factual or authoritative statements about Josh. He is both responding to Peter and adding the dimension of context to the dialogue. The fight that the family brought into the room gradually is translated into Peter's legitimate expression of feelings.

PETER: And it's time you grew up. You don't bother to work on your own problems! So we have to drop everything to help you twenty-four hours a day. I am sick of it and sick of you.

THERAPIST: You've really got to get this across. You are afraid that Josh doesn't understand that you need things to change. Josh, what do you think of what your father is saying?

Most of the time, in fact, Peter was loving and very available to his son, but he had also long complained that his son would do anything to prevent his saying no or withdrawing when he had nothing to give. When tired or not feeling well and blamed by Josh by not helping him, Peter would sometimes turn from loving attention to furious blaming. Linda found it easier to meet Josh's demands, but was quick to anger at any signs of her husband withdrawing from or blaming their son. Josh, usually good-natured and loving to his parents, could also become furious and profane when frustrated or left to his own resources.

Peter's individual frustration has as large an impact on Josh and Linda as their reaction has on him. Part of the process of the therapy that evening and in other meetings was to pay attention to the way change in Peter would affect his wife and son. We also discussed how

Peter might be expressing a change in the family development in which more responsibility would be handed over to Josh. A family crisis, however ungraceful, can be an attempt to open a door to change. Peter's need for change in the way the family members supported each other had validity; it was also true that he received much support during crises with his own health problems that he was not acknowledging in his current, emotionally aroused state. In this situation, as in many others, the therapist is aware that the conditions Peter is protesting were co-created and maintained by his own words and actions. Concepts from structural family therapy (Minuchin 1974, to be described in Chapter 3) help the empathic therapist: he is aware that a transition usually takes place when a child reaches Josh's age. Often first signalled by a fight, the transfer of responsibility and eventually authority must take place between parents and child. This awareness, while not expressed, allows the therapist to have confidence that a family, though in distress, is moving an important direction.

Eventually, the therapist spent five minutes alone with each family member to give them an opportunity to be heard without setting the others off. (This is one of many ways in which a therapist may facilitate a transition between intense interaction and individual reflection and integration.) The family then reconvened for calmer talk, in which Peter continued to insist that the family needed to change but with less accusation. Josh was given an opportunity to speak, which revealed more about his feelings of responsibility to help his parents with their marriage. Linda conceded Peter's right to say no to Josh, but also said that Peter as well as Josh expects her always to say yes, which she almost always does. She was also able to express her own grievance at not being able to come home from her difficult job without running into a fight.

In this case, the family members were able to express their individual frustrations in a setting in which feelings were allowed *but not treated as objective facts* with which to shame other family members. In the individual appointment that followed this session, Peter reported that each person felt heard and no longer under attack. In helpful dialogue, individual perceptions can be allowed to emerge side by side rather than in opposition to each other (Senge 1990). Furthermore, the expression of emotion in a safe, empathic setting allows for individual issues to be acknowledged and a new stage in family development to be named. Among new patterns emerging were the following:

- Peter can say that he doesn't want to take care of Josh in the same way without Josh being shamed for wanting the level of attention and support he was used to.
- Linda can signal that she doesn't want to be a witness to the kind of fighting she usually lives with and sorts out with great effort. By bringing her family trouble into the therapy, she was beginning to withdraw from the role of peacemaker.
- Josh is able to have a voice about the stresses he finds in living with his parents. He also can look for reassurance that his essential relationship with his father will endure even while its customs change.

Family therapy in which a therapist translates individual client feelings and thoughts allows a fight to become a dialogue and opens up the possibility of a higher level of family functioning. A family therapist's goal of facilitating transition from one stage to another is enhanced by a person-centred interest in hearing everyone out.

Conclusion

Chapter 1 has focused on the challenges all relationship therapists face, which lend themselves to a person-centred approach integrated with many resources from varied systems therapy traditions. Therapists must pay attention to clients' unique goals while offering multi-directional empathy, understanding of the ways couple and family processes interact with individual perception and a willingness to facilitate the process actively. Centred on Carl Rogers' core conditions for effective therapy, a person-centred approach suggests a life-long commitment to a 'way of being' (Rogers 1980) that can be integrated with the skills and knowledge required by couple and family therapy. Each therapist must find a way for the client experience of empathy and acceptance to appear in the midst of vigorous dialogue under stress. Chapter 2 continues the reflection on the integration of therapists' personal attitudes with client-centred skills with a description of six practices of a relationship therapist.

2

The Tasks of a Relationship Therapist

All my career, I have felt if I could answer the questions 'What is my purpose in the meeting? How can I be helpful?' then the clients would be strengthened in their ability to accept themselves and take initiatives in their own lives. In this chapter I describe six tasks, often revised over several years, which sustain my attitude and actions. Readers are invited to reflect on how their practices may parallel and differ from the following:

- Actively seek to understand and show acceptance of each person present.
- Provide structure for the sessions.
- Ask for, clarify and refer back to each person's purpose in being in the session.
- Sustain the conviction that each person is attempting to actualize themselves.
- Exercise a teaching function.
- Practise consistent non-defensiveness.

I am going to look at each of these tasks in turn and in doing so explore some of the practical issues that typically crop up in the course of family therapy.

Client Characteristics and Needs

Clients can be found in my waiting room slumped in exhaustion and/or boredom, excited at the opportunity to meet, eager to please, eager to make others sorry for not pleasing, fearful, hopeful, angry or impatient to get home and watch television or return to text-messaging their friends. They are always unpredictable in their actions. What is predictable, however, is that their initial behaviour does not accurately depict their reasons for being present, their level of motivation or their ability to initiate or cooperate with the change process.

Writing of his couple therapy and expressing a common therapist finding, Richard Stuart (1980) said that the client who openly wanted the marriage to continue still had some doubts about its worth, and the person who apparently wanted the marriage to end often had some ambivalence about its hopelessness. Similarly, teens in a power struggle with their parents may also have an unacknowledged hope that their parents stay engaged with them; their parents may have an unspoken affection for signs of their children's originality and a drive to take charge of their own lives. Making my own behaviour predictable offers a steadiness in which client expression, connection and variability may flourish.

Family Therapy as 'a humble sensible field'

A clear set of practices provides a balance between consistency and permission to adapt. The best therapy has structure enough to support clients in their unique expressive style without threatening the psychological safety of their loved ones. The structure must allow for freedom, responsiveness, inclusion, ownership and creation of meanings that cannot be predicted in advance. The relationship therapist takes for granted the task of correcting their own imbalance. You have to be a strong enough presence to allow a new dialogue to take place among family members and open enough to let them and their own solutions take centre stage. Lynn Hoffman (1998: 146) has written of her hope that family therapy would be 'a humble sensible field' and that is the purpose of this job description.

The six practices that are the focus of this chapter apply to a general awareness of who you are as a therapist and what are the boundaries of your responsibilities and expected and permitted activities. A personal set of tasks and boundaries is also a tool for finding your way at a difficult moment in a session. You ask yourself: Is what I am doing congruent? Or, at less promising moments, Does this work make any sense at all? Is it appropriate? If not, what can I do, right now, that would be congruent and appropriate?

Practice 1: Actively Seek to Understand and Show Acceptance of Each Person Present

At the beginning of every session I welcome each person separately. After the first session, I often offer a check-in that asks what has been important to them since we last met and invite them to say what they most want to talk about. As a matter of practice, I invite everyone into conversation with their family group and me. If, however, I find that one person is there unwillingly and/or somehow indicates discomfort in being expected to talk, I make a point of emphasizing each person's freedom not to speak as well as to speak. For example, I dread a mother telling an already unhappy young person, 'Come on Bill, speak to the man! That's what you're here for.' Freedom of speech is at the heart of relationship therapy. Also, despite what his mother said, I *don't* know what her son is here for.

The therapist never forgets two things:

- Individuals notice whether you can hear them and validate them or not.
- They are there in order to be in better conversation with their significant others, however argumentatively they may behave.

Successful relationship therapy is truly client centred: you adapt to clients who, for the most part, expect a therapist to orient and guide them. Some clients are ready from the beginning to talk with one another, to listen and show signs of being able to understand each other. Some other clients need the therapist to ask questions or otherwise give them a chance to get into the therapeutic conversation. Here are examples of seeking to understand and show acceptance of each person present:

- Each person gives an answer to: 'Why are you here and what would you like to get out of the therapy?' or a variation: 'What happened that led you to decide that you would want to come in for family (or couple) therapy?' The therapist practises active listening and attempts to understand each person's unique situation: 'So it comes down to fighting. You would really like to be able to talk but lately, it seems as though whenever you try to talk about something important, you just have to fight. Is that everyone's experience all the time or just sometimes?'

- With children, especially those under 11 and with some slightly older, I may say: 'I would like to find out what it is like in this family.' (Standing up and moving to four corners of the room) 'Over here is the happy section of the room: when you come over here, I would like each of you to tell me and each other what it's like when you are happy in this family. Over here is the worried or fearful side of family life: when you come over here I would like each of you to say what you are worried or scared about. Over here is the angry side … Over here is the sad side …' Families often use this simple device, influenced by the choreography modelled by family therapy founding mother Virginia Satir (1972, introduced in Chapter 1), as a vehicle to put their concerns into words.

- Multi-directional partiality or being on everyone's side at once may require explanation so that clients are not alienated by perceived attention to their apparent adversary. It can sometimes be useful for the therapist is to clarify their intention to *understand each perspective without joining in implied or explicit disapproval of others*. 'I am going to be listening to the parent side of this thing for a while. Do you understand that I will be listening, in a few minutes, to the kid side of this too?' It is also important for the therapist to be aware that, without intending it, their empathy for one person can be enthusiastic and for another can be parsimonious. Frequent client feedback, in writing or orally at the end of sessions, and a non-defensive attitude are important elements in the practice of relationship therapy. We do not always 'understand but always seek to understand' (Goolishian and Anderson 1992).

The therapist can show understanding for each person's feelings as well as conjecture what it is like for the family as a whole. When parents come with a teenager, I always say, 'There are two ways we can do this: I could meet with each of you individually, or we can all just start out together and see where we go.' Giving clients the choice of first individual contact or first contact as a whole is an important sign of respect and deference. It also is an important choice for clients' comfortableness. Some kids definitely want to start with a family meeting; others are very determined not to speak openly until they have connected individually with the therapist. Most therapies with adolescents tend to be a mixture of individual, parent and whole family therapy (Taffel 2008). I will return to these issues in more depth in Chapter 8, which focuses on therapy with children and adolescents.

Case Example 2.1: Respect and Accountability

A young mother, Kathleen wants and needs validation of her philosophy of parenting:

> The children deserve respect the way that we do. They are just little people. Even if you don't like what they are doing, you can't just raise your voice and order them to stop. You have to talk with them and listen to them. And if you do they will work it out with you.

In the same conversation, her husband Barry says:

> You ask them to do something in a really nice way. They say 'OK' and then they ignore what you ask. You come back ten minutes later and nothing has been done. Before you know, it is long after their bedtime and no one has moved a bit. Then I get mad and they listen and then Kathleen comes in and defends them and then we have a fight in front of them.

The therapist may want to be a parent like Kathleen and may remember having a parent like Barry (or vice versa), but their job is to meet each of them without excluding the other. A therapist might say:

> Barry feels that really strongly. The kids have to listen. Who will they become if they don't listen to reasonable requests? You are kind of on the accountability side of things. Would that be the right word? Kathleen, however, can't hear angry talk to her children without feeling they are being disrespected. You really believe that the kids never deserve a raised voice whatever they do or don't do. You are more on the respect side of things. I also think Kathleen really hates angry voices. *(The therapist knows this because he knows about her family-of-origin experience, to be described in Chapter 3 as well as Barry's.)* I think Barry really hates it when the kids seem not to be listening.

In the course of this particular conversation each person, being heard, became more able to hear the other. Barry did feel that Kathleen's philosophy was the better one and that indeed he had to work to let go of the habits his own parents modelled. He also needed her to get off his back so that he could get off the kids' backs in his own way.

Kathleen said that she needed to let Barry and the children work it out themselves more rather than jumping in. She also realized that she could land on Barry with her raised voice the same way she thought he landed on the kids. As important was for him to hear how deeply felt her ideas about their children were. She was not interested in being permissive but in being respectful.

It will usually emerge that one client evokes more natural sympathy in the therapist than another. The therapist's task is to remain curious and open to understanding and accepting the client who seems most distant or even difficult. In fact, it may be that the therapist needs to make a greater effort to connect with the person with whom they feel least affinity, as Blow and Sprenkle suggest (2007) in their studies of common factors in successful therapy. It is important that therapists do not view one client as the one with the greater emotional needs and therefore relegate a partner, parent or child to the role of supporter, adversary or bystander. For example, a wife who feels emotionally unsupported is not more the client than a husband who appears unresponsive or rigid; a child who feels criticized is not a more important client than a parent who is absorbed in disapproval and anxiety.

Some clients have little tolerance for negative feedback, disagreement or another person's receiving attention. This may be specific to one moment or one session and require sensitive facilitation. For example, a woman who had detected her husband in relapse of his gambling addiction told the therapist: 'Let him do the talking. I have nothing to say.' When her husband spoke, however, she would quickly interrupt him with strong statements or accusatory questions. After several repetitions of this the therapist said simply: 'It really seems important for you to have the floor today. There will be plenty of time for more back and forth later.' And, indeed, in later sessions the client was able to take turns with her husband. Some other clients set each other off so much that I have to offer a structure to let any exchange take place. Therapists may have to insist that they be allowed the role of translator and buffer in order to make any conversation possible, for example when clients address their remarks to the therapist, who then expresses a less inflammatory translation to their partner or family member. On rare occasions the clients are never able to tolerate listening to the other without interruption and need referral to another modality.

The family therapist creates safety for conversations to take place that, when they are over, allow persons to proceed as individuals on their life paths without having to hurt each other or cut each other off.

Practice 2: Provide Structure for the Sessions

As Gottman (1999) comments, 'Couple or family therapy with an inactive therapist can be unhelpful, even harmful, and has no support in research on couples' therapy.' Structure, however, does *not* mean 'directiveness (teaching, advice giving, interpreting)' (Butler and Bird 2000).

A couple beginning therapy with me complained that their last, unhelpful therapist 'didn't offer us any structure'. I don't think they meant that they wished she had told them what to do. They meant that the therapy didn't seem responsive to the goals they expressed. (Research on the therapist/client alliance emphasizes the importance not only of rapport with the therapist, but also of client-experienced alignment of goals (Cooper 2008; Sprenkle et al. 2009). Structure is not about therapist control; at its best, it is, rather, therapist responsiveness to clients' needs and intentions, expressed or not expressed. Clients need to be able to talk about important matters without driving each other silent and/or out of the room or house. Box 2.1 reflects on the therapist's decision to use structure.

Box 2.1: Person-Centred Therapy and Structure

Can structure be client centred? Carl Rogers chose client control of structure in his therapy and group leadership – although he asserted that as a group member he could speak for what he wished without imposing it (Kirschenbaum and Henderson 1990). He (Rogers 1967) contended that the client was the expert and 'unless I had a need to demonstrate my own cleverness and learning, I would do better to rely upon the client for the direction of movement in the process'. Thirty-five years of experience with couples and families have taught me the following:

- Without structure, the family process that is causing distress will control the therapy session. The dominating will dominate; the emotionally cut-off will withdraw; the emotionally expressive will feel unheard; the overlooked will continue to be invisible. The therapist's empathy, congruence and unconditional positive regard as well as clients' feelings and thoughts will be unnoticed.
- All structure that is offered, however, must exist in support of client freedom to speak and be listened to; dialogue that allows new experience of self and one another; collaboration on shared goals and acknowledgement of differing goals.

- Structure is offered in relation to client goals and yields to client clarification of changing wishes. As clients become secure in their ownership of therapy, they become more and more the directors of the therapy. (In Case Example 1.1, Linda decided that Peter's individual session needed to be a family session.)

Some family and couple therapists disempower clients by too much structure; others fail to make the therapy safe with supportive guidance. Each of us needs supervision to be welcoming facilitators in whose presence clients do work that only they can direct.

Much structure is common sense: people take turns, everyone has a chance to agree on the topic to be discussed before we go into it. The following are predictable elements in the sessions that I facilitate:

- The therapist explains the general format of the therapy and, if appropriate, relates it to the reason for the couple's attending.
- Each person has an opportunity to say what they would like to talk about before a conversation is launched that includes as close to a consensus topic as possible. An agenda may be set: 'We will talk about this first, then this, then this etc.'
- The therapist actively invites quieter people to talk if they choose and more talkative people to make room for others' responses. This is done with respect and openness to client comfort with such prompting.
- The therapist takes on the role of translator or coach if an angry conversation turns hostile or one client seems flooded with reaction when another speaks.
- The therapist may comment on the process as it unfolds and invite client reflection on how the dialogue is working or not working. For example, the therapist may ask if their general dialogue is allowing each to feel heard or if they would like to practise 'Speaker/Listener', a process of taking turns speaking and being an active listener for the other (to be discussed in more detail in Chapter 5).
- When couples have had a particularly intense session, I sometimes invite them to move from their chairs to other seats in the five or ten minutes before the end of a session. Without my having to ask them explicitly, they fall into an observer mode and we discuss what took place. One couple, who can fight quite bitterly and arrive quickly at 'I'm right/you're wrong' impasses, easily switch into a more humorous mode and look at each other, even making well-received

comments like 'I'm the only one who would put up with you' or 'Divorce would be a lot of trouble'.

- The therapist keeps time very carefully and reserves the last five minutes for summarizing the events of the session, checking that someone has not been left unexpectedly hurt or disempowered, acknowledging agreements reached and issues unresolved, and asking if and when to schedule a next session. Letting the time end randomly – 'Oh, I see our time is up. Too bad' – can leave clients unnecessarily stressed and pessimistic because of one provocative or discouraging remark. (No therapist is always able to keep an angry family from leaving on an angry note, but taking responsibility for checking how people feel at the end of a session is a form of caring.)
- It is increasingly my practice to invite each person to share an appreciation for words or actions in the session or preceding week. This is not a random, cheerful, 'always look on the bright side of life' idea; it is a structure that allows overlooked strengths to enter the room. (Both couple therapy – Chapters 5 and 6 – and family therapy with young people are enlivened by attention to usually neglected strengths.) It means inviting clients into the important work of noticing one another outside of their rigid mutual characterizations. Such an extremely simple practice can provide an important way to discover and acknowledge the kinds of change that will shift the nature of the family interaction. It can be a most powerful way for clients to motivate each other towards taking individual responsibility for change in the system, as I will discuss in Chapter 3.

A note about conflict and structure: I have never found it helpful for couples or family members to 'fight it out', 'go off on each other' or otherwise have a free-for-all conflict. Clients feel resentful and discouraged if they are allowed to express or forced to receive hostile, attacking words from one another. In many couples or families, such volleys will break out. Sometimes I wait to see if the clients can contain or otherwise channel their angry feelings into real communication. If the conflict heads towards the irrational and hostile, I take responsibility for asking their assistance in making sense out of the anger that is expressed. 'Let me do my job,' I sometimes say. My 'job' is to facilitate dialogue, not sit silent in the face of what could easily become abuse. (Clients are allowed to divorce each other, separate from each other, not agree with or even dislike each other; they are not allowed to abuse each other in my presence.) It is not that clients do not have to say things that are strong, negative and definitely hurt feelings. It is that their expression should serve the purpose of clarifying unheard emotions and unmet needs rather than attacking or otherwise diminishing their loved ones.

Practice 3: Ask for, Clarify and Refer Back to Each Person's Purpose in Being in the Session

Relationship therapy can be an emotional experience: being in the presence of their intimate others often produces reactivity, sensitivity and vulnerability that can overwhelm the ability to communicate well.

> Whenever clients become anxious, argumentative or lost in a monologue, *reference to each person's stated reason for being there enables them to become present to the dialogue at hand.* For example, the therapist may ask: 'Is this it? Is this the kind of dreadful moment you were describing?' (O'Leary and Johns 2007)

Therapist questions directed towards understanding and validation can soothe by allowing client thoughtfulness to co-exist with strong feelings. 'What is it that you would most like to get across right now?' a therapist may ask an angry, frustrated client, using a phrase from couple therapist Dan Wile (1993). Clients are often in therapy because they are frustrated and they may be calmed by the opportunity to translate feelings into words *that are heard.* It can be useful in the middle of a session to ask: 'Are we talking about what you had hoped we would talk about?' This not only invites the client to engage more intentionally, but also models a skill needed at home: to break into a conversation based on angry reactions and tune into a conversation in which people can understand and be understood.

Among the questions I may use are the following:

- 'What do you want (this person, these persons) to understand before we leave this session?' Such a question also encourages client curiosity, not only about what others know and think about them, but about what they themselves hold essential and, in many cases, are feeling beneath the level of argument and struggle.
- 'If we were really getting somewhere in this therapy, what would be the first sign of that happening?' (This is a question derived from solution-oriented therapy, to be described below in Box 2.3.)
- 'What is it that (this person, these persons) doesn't know about what you are thinking and feeling? What would they say, if they faced the

situation you are in right now? Who is it who would be least surprised by what you are going through?' (This kind of question is influenced by the 'circular questions' of the Milan group; Boscolo et al. 1987; Hoffman 2002; see also Box 2.2.)

- 'How does discussion of this topic affect you all? Is this the important thing to be talking about?' (These questions invite client responsibility for the direction of the therapy, giving permission for a change of subject and encouragement for more direct communication.)

All sessions, especially the first, invite clients to say what they want. I take notes of what people say specifically and at intense times in the therapy read back their own words with the question: 'Does this connect with what you are looking for or are you aware that you want something different now?' The client is invited to reflect on awareness of different, more important intentions or to make the connection between their behaviour and their stated intention. Sometimes the clients are so immersed in the emotional moment that they cannot step out of it. The therapist may make their own empathic conjecture for the client to accept or reject. For example: 'You feel so concerned about your son's safety that it almost feels as if you would do anything to keep him from danger. It is very hard for you to listen to him at all when you think he is taking risks. Is that it?' Relationship therapy is both emotional experience and reflection. It is also the translation of thoughts expressed through 'hard language' – e.g. angry, coercive, threatening, accusatory – into softer language – 'I statements' or expression of softer emotions such as fear, attachment, caring (Johnson and Greenberg 1994).

The therapist stays closely tuned to whether the use of session time is congruent with the client's purposes. Such awareness is a compass that can set the therapy in the right direction when participants are lost.

Practice 4: Sustain the Conviction that All Clients Are Attempting to Actualize Themselves

It is an act of hope to come in for therapy. The couple or family are looking for something to happen by which they can restore something that they had or create something they hoped for. They want to 'get sorted' so that they can find a way to proceed. Expectancy or hope or the 'placebo effect' accounts for 15 per cent of client change, according to meta-studies on outcomes of successful therapy (Asay and Lambert 1999; Cooper 2008).

In a person-centred approach, motivation is perceived as present in the client; the therapist listens as the client searches through motivation that has been lost and may be found again if the client can feel safe to be themselves. Each client has motivation that can be overlooked or invalidated by their loved ones. The therapist offers 'empathic conjectures' about what each client is expressing (Moser and Johnson 2008).

This therapist has learned and continually struggles to remember that he cannot, through whatever cleverness he possesses, get someone else to change. In family therapy such efforts inevitably confuse clients, make the therapist the ally of one or more clients against the other, and don't help people change successfully the family's success, unity, use of virtues and problem-solving ability.

Therapists can be of help insofar as they normalize each person's part in the conversation. That is, they connect events of this client group with what would be expected of most people in the same developmental situation. The therapist interviews family members in the face of their predicaments, feeling the emotions appropriate to the many sides of each issue. I may say to a parent: 'Parents feel they have to get their kids to go to school. I don't know any way around this. They can sympathize greatly with their kid's frustration but never feel good about their not going to school.' I can say to a teen: 'I think you know parents can never not let their kids go to school. Is there any way that your dad can be there for you without saying you don't have to go to school?' I can say to the whole family: 'Are we here for a family meeting about what the family can do when a kid hasn't been able to go to school more than twice in the first week? What does each of you think should be done?'

Therapists never deny the central issues, even while they empathize with the divergent thoughts about those issues. A child can't bear to go to school; a parent can't allow him not to. The various attempts at resolution are validated by the therapist while the family searches for a solution.

Some therapies, as in Box 2.2, define dysfunctional patterns in a family or couple and prescribe an intervention that breaks an impasse and allows change to flow. Person-centred therapy avoids the position of director, but may express similar imaginative, intuitive or even humorous perspectives on relationship predicaments.

Box 2.2: American Strategic Therapy and the Milan Group

Strategic therapists such as Jay Haley and Cloé Madanes have offered brief, prag-matic, imaginative interventions to free families and couples from patterns that kept them from progressing in their development and living lives of 'richness and complexity' (Haley 1973). This approach can be studied in detail in the work of Madanes (1981) and Haley (1982); more recently one might read Mitrani and Perez (2003) for an overview of the theory and practice of this approach.

Strategic therapy, a directive approach (Haley and Richeport-Haley, 2007), could not differ more from a person-centred approach in philosophy and in the self-description of their leading figures. Good strategic therapists are, however, poetic, metaphorical and dedicated to a view of human potential that is akin to Carl Rogers' actualizing tendency. Strategic therapists look for ways to reframe an issue so that clients' strengths are evoked and their doubts about change are bypassed.

In a therapist exposed to strategic thinking, clients have someone who can take advantage of an outside observer's perspective. Such therapists can see patterns; see the language of events; make educated guesses about communication that is non-verbal and implicit. Strategic therapists offer a wealth of practical experience about connecting with clients as real people rather than experts in therapy.

Strategic therapists attempt to influence a system through a small shift in verbal or behavioural attention rather than a lengthy, therapist-centred analysis. They offer eccentric ideas that are responsive to the irrational aspects of all human life. For example, Cloé Madanes frequently asks parents to focus on correcting only three of their teenager's behaviours. Practising this deceptively reasonable direc-tive opens the door to awareness of how a parent may be in a continuous, unend-ing state of criticism towards their beloved child (Madanes 2009). Under other circumstances, they may offer the reframing that apparently bad communication serves a purpose that has to do with developmental needs for separation and privacy.

An approach that developed from similar sources to strategic therapy – that is, Gregory Bateson, Donald Jackson and others at the Mental Research Institute (Hoffman 2003) – is the work of the Milan group (Boscolo et al. 1987). This group of therapists developed the concept of 'positive attribution' (Palazzoli et al. 1981), in which seemingly dysfunctional behaviour may be relabelled as an attempt to be helpful. This relinquishing of blame and worry may paradoxically eliminate the need for the behaviour. (There may be a connection between the effect of this inter-vention and the way in which person-centred unconditional acceptance can lead to a change in behaviour.) The Milan Group developed 'circular questions', 'built on sensitivity to many kinds of differences … designed to show the hidden connections between seemingly unrelated events' (Hoffman 2003: 92). Circular questions create 'curiosity' and 'perturbation' in the system that lead to change and use of client resources.

A person-centred therapist influenced by these approaches to therapy may do the following:

- Look for, discover or highlight paradoxes.
- Notice and encourage awareness of unintended consequences, especially positive ones, e.g. 'Here you are, having had the fight of your lives, and yet you seem closer and more at ease with each other.'
- Discover overlooked humour.
- Discover under-emphasized aspects of their role.
- Use imagination to highlight goals.

The following are phrases that I have used because of my exposure to strategic therapy. Each statement has two characteristics: it is an accurate statement on its own merits – a legitimate way of telling the truth – and it also offers a paradoxical perspective and speaks to an unacknowledged, unspoken side of an issue. What is different from conventional strategic therapy is that the family is invited to consider, contradict and otherwise join in a different form of reflection. Note the question that is connected with the observation.

- 'Am I wrong that everyone here seems to see you as powerful even though you don't think you have any influence at all?'
- 'You are in the role of the family spokesperson for the sadder truths of life. Do you wonder sometimes if other people need to talk more about what they are sad about? Who in the family, besides you, knows the most about being sad?' (This is the circular questioning of the Milan group (Hoffman 2003: 192–3).
- 'The one thing that is *not* allowed to happen is that you finish something on time – like finish a year of college. If something happens to you, naturally you are supposed to drop out of school; you must never finish. That's your job, which you will do no matter what anyone says or does. Of course you have, in fact, finished lots of things, but doesn't it feel like all the dragons in the family come out when you are about to become more independent?' (A brief note on humour: this last statement reflects a style that comes naturally to me. There is absurdity in the inevitability of certain frustrating patterns: as if failure really were a job that one does. I make such statements, laughing with the clients at a repeating story rather than at them. If they buy into the feeling that their life seems unjustly determined, they may become empowered to rebel by being more mindful and intentional. I never use humour; I discover it. If the

client doesn't seem more relaxed or empowered by humour, I drop it.)

- 'Your problems as parents are the problems of excellence: you both feel great urgency about doing the right thing for your children. You can't seem to get along with each other at all, but aren't your problems better than those of neglect and not caring? I guess the question is: Can you support each other at all in what you are trying to do?'
- 'What is the right amount of fighting these kids need? What would be lost if they stopped fighting altogether?'

Practice 5: Exercise a Teaching Function

We may not feel like teachers, but our clients hope to learn something. Writing about couples, Carl Rogers deplored the lack of information available about relationships and the raising of children, as we see in his book *Becoming Partners* (1972), in which he presented the results of interviews with middle-class couples in a variety of heterosexual relationships, reflections on his reading about couples and the personal story of his then 47-year relationship with his wife Helen – a relationship that ended with her death after 61 years of marriage (Kirschenbaum 2007). Rogers did not think highly of the existing literature on how to be married, saying that it consisted of 'manuals and surveys'. He sought to capture what relationships felt like from 'the inside'; as always, he paid attention to each person's 'experience' of the relationship. He also wrote that couples entered into relationships with less training about this important part of life, especially a marriage with children, than they would have for much less significant enterprises. He advocated more research on what life was like with couples, more preparation, more knowledge about how to communicate, how to listen and about other people's experience of marriage. (See Chapter 5, Box 5.1, for an example of the research now available.) In his own life he felt very fortunate to have been assisted by a physician who encouraged his enquiry about his wife's, hitherto unspoken, experience in their sexual life and taught them needed information about the physical aspect of sexuality, as well as ways to communicate that made their sexual connection satisfying and mutual.

As a teacher, Rogers evolved in an ever more student-centred direction. He did not, however, just leave students alone without making resources available. Invariably, he brought in books, papers, prepared lectures, reading lists and other materials. His trust of his students was shown in always letting them decide which, if any, resources they chose to use (Rogers 1969).

As a couple and family therapist, I follow his lead: making available any resources I have – techniques, homework, research information – but leaving clients the choice of what to use. In my own work with couples and families, I am also sometimes like Rogers' physician, suggesting enquiries that clients have not thought to make. Sometimes, too, I offer information that seems otherwise not available to them.

Among many things I may say to clients in the course of therapy are the following:

- 'Guess which gender tends to be comfortable in conflict (as long as there is no danger of violence) and which gender tends to avoid intense conversations in which anger may be expressed?' Clients invariably and correctly answer female to the former and male to the latter. With same-sex couples usually one member of a couple is eager for contact, even about negative subjects, while the other person tries to avoid intense conversations.
- Around 66 per cent of couples experience significant distress after the birth of a first child. Among many reasons for this is that each person feels they are no longer a priority for the other.
- Parents often divide themselves into one person who emphasizes accountability and another who emphasizes unconditional love. Most parents actually believe in both those aspects of relationships.
- Almost every couple who stay together long enough can discover differences in feelings about their sex life. Everyone has to keep learning about the other person as they change; no one finds that easy.

Almost all of these remarks are delivered in such a way that the clients can take them or leave them. They express intent to normalize the trouble a family is having, as well as to challenge the expectation that other people resolve predicaments easily. Clients often feel that their own behaviours are uniquely dysfunctional and live with the mistaken impression that most other people know how to handle the complexities of life better than they do. Therapists offer their knowledge as a resource and consider the clients as the final arbiters of what is relevant and what they choose to use.

For the most part, teaching is a client-centred process, not a hierarchical, expert-centred series of directives. The person-centred therapist privileges what clients are teaching themselves. I actively affirm clients' knowledge of what they need and their preferred ways of managing conversations. Each session produces data about the way life is at home; we all participate in evaluating what each session produces. When clients seem stuck and bogged down in argument, I may offer clipboards to the members of a family or a couple. 'What is it,' I ask them to write, 'that would be a sign that you are getting along better? What quality in your partner, child, parent or sibling would you see more of? Less of? What quality in you would your family see more of? What less of?' The tone of these questions is derived from solution-focused therapy, which educates by orienting clients towards describing the way their relationship is when it is hopeful and harmonious.

Box 2.3 describes the process of this type of therapy.

Box 2.3: Solution-Focused Therapy

Solution-focused therapy is a post-modernist therapy that emerged from the search for a brief therapy in a city clinic and is most identified with Steve de Shazer (1994) and Insoo Berg (Berg and Miller 1992), life and work partners for years at the Brief Family Therapy Center in Wisconsin. 'If this problem were solved next week, what do you think would have happened?' Is a hypnotic question that captures the heart of this approach. Solution-focused therapists allow clients to bypass the complexities of a problem and focus on the actions and beliefs that would support its resolution.

Intended to be brief and entirely client focused, this therapy, like narrative therapy, is centred on questions that change systems by allowing clients to conceptualize what their preferred relationships and future would look like. These include:

* Questions about change that clients have *already* initiated. It is always worth asking clients what they have tried since making the call for the appointment. Almost invariably, clients have started the process of change. Taking note of the efforts that clients are making outside of therapy directs the therapist's attention to the way the actualizing tendency is unfolding. This is a form of hypnotist-psychiatrist Milton Erickson's 'utilization' (Berg and Miller 1992); that is, the noticing and evocation of overlooked client resources in the resolution of client difficulties.
* Miracle questions, such as: 'While you are sleeping a miracle happens and the problem that brought you here is solved … What do you suppose will be the first small thing that will indicate to you tomorrow morning that there has been a miracle overnight and the problem that brought you here is solved? … What else?' (Berg and Miller 1992: 78). A related questions is: 'What would be different if you and your wife suddenly noticed you were getting along better?'
* Exception questions that, like White's 'unique outcomes', investigate times when desirable events happened unexpectedly or undesirable events unexpectedly fail to happen. For instance: 'Why did your son attend school all last week?'

Critics of this approach warn against imposing positive language that struggles with the clients' preferred way of expression. A person-centred therapist may add these questions to their repertoire of conversational possibilities even as they listen carefully to clients' expression of distress, fear and negative thinking.

In helpful therapy clients often learn the following:

- That their problems arise not out of deficiency, but out of one or more family members' attempt to grow. The expected stages of family development are implicitly and sometimes explicitly discussed in therapy.
- That arguments have their roots in core client needs that feel overlooked or thwarted, and in the desire to have their voices heard and significance acknowledged.
- That differences understood and accepted can contribute to harmony and differences denied or resisted account for much conflict and rejection.
- That the understanding of gender differences can help people take care of themselves and their loved ones more effectively.
- That having one or more children changes a couple's relationship for ever.
- That blending a family of two adults with children happens more easily and more successfully the more patient, open to learn from mistakes, respectful of boundaries and accepting of children's complex feelings a couple are willing to be.

For clients who identify themselves as liking to read or having car time in which to listen to CDs, I recommend a variety of books about relationships, conflict resolution, family-of-origin exploration and reconciliation, and parenting.

Practice 6: Practise Consistent Non-defensiveness

Non-defensiveness is a form of wisdom that allows a person not to take events personally, to be more interested in useful conversation than being right or seen as intelligent or powerful, and to be there for the other person rather than supporting one's own sense of importance. An attitude of not having to defend allows attention to be focused on what matters to the clients rather than on the therapist. It is this very attitude of freedom and curiosity that is useful to model to clients attempting change in their close relationships. Person-centred family therapist Ned Gaylin has written that 'accuracy in empathic reflections is sometimes over-rated, I think' (2008: 242). I couldn't agree more with his implication that clients' freedom to correct the therapist's understanding and comment on their behaviour strengthens the clients' comfort in and ownership of their own unique experiencing.

Therapists model acceptance of the normality of mistakes and an attitude of exploration rather than perfection. They admit mistakes readily, accept client concerns as legitimate and see misunderstandings as a normal part of conversation. John Gottman has said that couples who thrive have difficulties and even fights; they differ from distressed couples in their willingness to seek to repair and to allow others to repair actual or perceived injuries (Gottman et al. 2006).

Non-defensiveness is all the more important the more active and verbal you are. It is the other side of the coin of directivity. If you say or suggest something that is wrong in clients' eyes, you don't insist on proving you are right. On the contrary, you see their disagreement as a sign that they are claiming control over the therapy as well as their own lives. Frequent use of written client evaluations, immediately after the session as we will discuss in Chapter 4, allows for client freedom to report the impact of the session on them (as distinct from the therapist's assumptions and good intentions). For example, therapists, outside their awareness, may be seen as allying with their own gender. Defensiveness on this issue will almost certainly strengthen that perception.

Case Example 2.2: Therapist's Relationship Repair

At one point in therapy, Art mentioned having invited his wife, Barb, to take a walk just to talk, which was exactly what she had frequently asked him to do. When he pointed out this conscious attempt to show her influence on him, she brushed it aside and went on with her complaints as if he had not spoken. When I pointed that she had ignored this attempt to connect with her, she appeared not to take note and continued making her point about Art's lack of responsiveness to her. Somewhat more strongly than I intended and much more strongly than is a good idea, I confronted her about ignoring Art's attempt to fulfil her request. She heard me this time, but appeared confused and said that perhaps she was tired and that she was not herself during this session.

Our next session began with me bringing up our exchange and my concern that I had been critical of her rather than able to respond to where she was. *(It is always my practice to take responsibility for repairing an injury or resolving any misunderstanding that originates in my own words or behaviour.)* She readily agreed and said that she had considered not attending the current session: 'I was right back at home being criticized by my mother and sisters.' I encouraged her expression of her feelings about this as well as her impression of what I said and how I said it. She had felt ganged up on. (Art had in fact congratulated me on my helpfulness and insight!) She had been made to feel stupid, she told me. I did not think that she was stupid. I admitted that I had become caught up in making a point to her rather than understanding her. I did not use the point I had been making or anything about her as a reason or excuse for how I had acted. I had been critical and she had felt ganged up on. I apologized.

Barb accepted my apology with warmth and relief and said that it had cleared things up between us. She went on to say that Art rarely apologized to her in a way that felt so respectful. Art pointed out that he often apologized, but never got his apology accepted the way mine had been.

Barb pointed out the difference: 'Usually Art's apologies are accompanied by a criticism of me for having caused him to do what he was sorry for.'

Art replied thoughtfully, 'I'll have to think about that.'

Barb responded, looking at him, 'And I'm sorry if I don't always hear you when you say something kind.'

Moments when clients challenge the therapist or (more rarely) are upset with them can be seen as opportunities for client learning and growth. When the therapist is not defensive in these moments, clients can feel safe to speak frankly about what is most important to them. In so doing, they may feel able to risk speaking openly and clearly to their loved ones.

Conclusion

All six of the tasks described in this chapter call on the confidence, patience, maturity and wisdom of the therapist. Since most therapists, however bright and well trained, are ordinary people with their own troubles and limitations, they need to find consistent practices, not only to bring out their best but to be vigilant towards the possible appearances of their worst.

These six practices refer to both attitude and behaviour. Relationship therapy requires structure as well as empathic attention to each person present. In response to clients' explicit and implied needs, the therapist both takes responsibility and turns responsibility over to clients in relation to their goals and ability to tolerate the demands of dialogue. Relationship therapy also requires therapist awareness of and management of their own sometimes unnoticed needs to be helpful, in control and, perhaps especially, right. Therapist security and confidence in their own purpose in therapy allow them to be open to clients' unique needs and possibilities. Chapter 3 will discuss a person-centred reflection on systems thinking.

3

Staying Personal while Thinking Systems

Sometimes client systems are untangled by returning to careful listening to individual frames of reference; sometimes client predicaments are resolved by a wider lens systems perspective. In this chapter I will discuss systems thinking, an elusive concept to be rediscovered and newly applied every time a therapist of any orientation or level of experience meets a couple or family. Chapter 4 will continue my discussion of a theoretical base by presenting Roger's six conditions as a systems intervention. This chapter offers a variety of perspectives on systems thinking, including:

- Presenting many levels of reframing compatible with the practice of an authentic therapist.
- Describing typical rules that make a system dysfunctional.
- Giving an example of the utility of genograms in a person-centred practice.
- Illustrating ways in which a person-centred approach can facilitate a more human-friendly system.

I discuss the implications of common factors found in all systems therapies for a person-centred practice and close with case examples of beginning, middle and ending person-centred relationship therapy.

Systems Thinking

A couple came in to report substantial improvement in their relationship after one therapy visit. 'Funny thing is,' one of them said, 'neither of us thinks we have changed ourselves, but we both think that the other has changed for the better.' Because they thought the other had or even was willing to change, each perceived a different relationship world and so became different themselves. Their willingness to come for therapy and the therapist's listening without judgement had broken a spell that had troubled them: their system had changed.

A systems therapist always meets a person in context. Asked what systems thinking means to him, family therapist Jim Thomas replied, 'No client ever enters my office alone.' In one case, more fully described below, Carolyn came to see me by herself because she was 'angry' and needed to decide whether she could get over it enough to continue to live with Gene, her husband, or if she should leave him. While listening to her feelings, I was aware of the untold story of her life with Gene, of his perceptions about the state of the relationship and of the systems that have an impact on them, now summed up by the feeling 'angry'. Individual therapy eventually became couple therapy: she chose to work on her feelings in the context of the living relationship in which they emerged.

Systems thinking refers to the awareness that all individual thoughts, feelings and actions take place in an interdependent web that both influences them and is influenced by them. The important meaning of systems is that the causes and the resolution of issues are not contained only in what individuals feel – although being allowed to say what you feel is an important gateway to meaning – but also in the *wider field* of thoughts, feelings and experiences and developmental and social events that form the context of those feelings. A family or couple system is an organization that helps a small group achieve its mission: sustaining basic life needs, allowing children to grow up safely, facilitating life in all its stages, meeting needs for attachment, esteem and personal development. Seventeenth-century poet John Donne said it best:

> No man is an island
> Entire of itself.
> Each is a piece of the continent,
> A part of the main … (Donne 1624)

Human Life Is Individual Choices *and* a Reaction to Systemic Pressures

Everything said or done is not just a by-product of the inner life of the individual client, but is an expression of an ongoing dialogue that has been taking place between many participants over many generations (Rober 2005). Person-centred therapist and philosopher Peter Schmid has said that the person *is* dialogue, with an inner life connected with a lifetime of interaction (2006). In our everyday language, people 'set each other off', they 'don't let each other off the hook', they 'push each other's buttons', they say 'don't get me started' or 'he shut me right down', they 'get in each other's face', 'rub each other up the wrong way' or 'get each other off on the wrong foot'.

The self-concept of each family member is, in part, affected by the relational system into which they were born and in which they live; at the same time, the relational field is changed by any change in the self-concept of one family member. The path to change includes understanding and connecting with the individual while making sense out of how they affect and are affected by the wider system. We live by our perceived individual decisions, but what we do reflects the emotional field in which we live. We seem to ourselves to be living by our own choices, but seen from outside we may also be living out rigid patterns.

For example, a woman brings up an incident of her husband's concealed intimate 'online' relationship before their marriage at the same time as she and her husband discuss their genograms (see below for an example of a genogram and its relevance to another couple). Her own mother and grandmother had 'cheating' husbands, as did her sister and sister-in-law. Could my clients be free of these recurring struggles or would they be destined to repeat the same patterns?

Bringing up dreaded family history in the context of current problems is a form of 'making the covert, overt' (Anonymous 1978); that is, making unspoken cross-generational fears explicit so that they may be evaluated for validity in the present. The couple were able to discuss ways in which their experience and character may allow them to differ from old family patterns.

Carl Rogers' 1960 dialogue with behaviourist researcher B. F. Skinner included his assertion that individuals always had the ability to choose; Skinner asserted that individuals only think that they choose while, in reality, they are directed by contingencies outside their awareness (Kirschenbaum and Henderson 1990). The person-centred relationship therapist lives in a world in which two things are true at the same time: we make our own choices *and* we live out dynamics of which we are not aware.

Like Rogers, the person-centred systems therapist facilitates individual awareness that is released from 'shoulds' and attempts to please and is enhanced by increased self-acceptance. They also encourage awareness of the pattern in which the individual lives and the emotional field that can discourage original thoughts and actions.

Elements of a Systems Perspective

Systems thinking usually involves awareness of power dynamics, repeating sequences of behaviour, the dialectic between explicit norms and descriptions and unspoken but more powerful implicit norms and behaviour. The therapist holds the awareness that everything that happens in the individual is reflective of what is in the field, and that the field is influenced by the individual's thoughts, feelings and actions. For example, a man feels insecure at the same time as his partner feels critical. If he asks her to help him feel more secure, she may become more critical. A woman feels unloved and lonely at the same time as a man feels controlled and trapped. If she asks him for more affection, he may become less available.

Systems thinkers are aware of the influence of developmental stages in the lives of adults as well as children and their effects on the emotional tone of a home. Historical family patterns, present extended families and friends, economic matters, the neighbourhood in which one lives, health, good luck and bad luck, and even, in Boston, Massachusetts, whether the baseball Red Sox are winning or in Manchester, England, whether United are having a good football season can influence the system. Most couples and families are strongly affected by the health, well-being, attitude and historical patterns of each partner's family of origin, as we will discuss below.

A classic and clear view of a systems approach has been provided by the work of Salvador Minuchin and structural family therapy, introduced in Box 3.1.

Box 3.1: Structural Family Therapy

Structural family therapy is most identified with Salvador Minuchin, still a family therapy sage at the age of 87. As the longtime director of the Philadelphia Child Guidance Center and a roving trainer over the last 50 years, Minuchin had a strong influence on such therapists as Marianne Walters, famous for integrating structural principles with respect for individuals; Jay Haley and Cloé Madanes, founders of strategic family therapy; Susan Johnson, co-founder of emotion-focused couple therapy; and Ron Taffel, whose work with the families of teenagers will be discussed in Chapter 8.

Structural family therapy pays attention to the way in which a family or couple organize themselves. Informed by a structural approach, a family therapist observes and responds to the rules, customs, organizational plan (explicit or, more often, implicitly assumed) and expected developmental tasks. A good family therapist is interested not just in how people feel or communicate, but also in the context in which they relate to one another (Mitrani and Perez 2003). Structural family therapy at its simplest takes for granted that some event, some transition, some change in hierarchy or boundaries has had an influence on the emotional field in which the family or couple are living. Family and couple therapy involves facilitating people not only in relation to one another, but also in relation to their situation, either an external entity that troubles their life or the habits of relating to each other that they have developed over time.

Among the dimensions that the structural approach attends to are:

- hierarchy and power affecting decision making and control;
- boundaries, which can be appropriately flexible, too rigid or too undefined;
- developmental tasks relating to the age and experiences of each family member;
- norms and expectations about children's behaviour;
- expectations about money, social life, religion, sexuality;
- expectations about involvement with and conformity to family-of-origin norms;
- roles of males and females in hierarchy, work distribution, responsibility and permission to change;
- the fact that every relationship is up against something that cannot be seen as caused by any one person. 'It is the objective situation you face not just the person,' Martin Buber said in his dialogue with Carl Rogers (Kirschenbaum and Henderson 1990). Structural family therapy allows clients to see the non-personal, non-intentional aspects of their relationship difficulties.

Structural family therapy has been known for being therapist centred, directive and oriented towards facilitating change in a system so that developmental progress may be made. Each problem or symptom is seen as the result of a system that is no longer adapting. The therapist functions as an organizational consultant, both clarifying ambiguous roles and normalizing the troubles besetting the family.

One influential technique from structural family therapy is the enactment; that is, a request that a family or couple demonstrate a problem from home in the therapy room. The therapist can advise, coach, comment or ask questions as the family live out their at-home reality. In more directive days, the therapist might tell a parent to take action – 'Get your children to stop fighting' – and then make suggestions as to how to do so. Enactments can also be part of a more collaborative process in which the therapist requests a short demonstration, then facilitates dialogue about each person's feelings, intentions and options. (See my description of how I use enactments in Chapter 1.)

Clients usually welcome enactments when they are offered along with other choices in references to their problems and goals. Even the slightest action about an at-home problem can, in the presence of a supportive facilitator, bring safe expression of emotion, awareness of underused skills and, sometimes, humour and community feeling.

Rules for a Dysfunctional Family System

Many clients have grown up with some or all of the following unspoken 'rules' and sometimes such rules are carried into the therapy session. The therapist must be understanding and responsive in the presence of these rules, while facilitating more open, trusting communication. The experience of a conversation without these rules can facilitate a change in the whole system. The rules are:

- Someone has to be wrong in order to have another person be right.
- Someone has to be emotionally blocked in order that another person is emotionally at peace.
- If a parent or partner is unable to meet someone's needs, the needs should not exist.
- A person is identified with the problem they bear without attention to other aspects of their character.
- Fear cannot be discussed as a dynamic, nor can self-pity, and therefore they must be projected on others.
- Negative, doubting, tragic, dependent, confused feelings will, if talked about, make things worse.

There are many paradigms of repetitive system deadlocks that are found in systems literature, for example in Lerner (1989):

- *Pursuer/distancer*: the more one person seeks closeness, the more the other seeks apartness and vice versa.
- *Over-functioning/under-functioning*: one person's taking responsibility contributes to another's withdrawal from responsibility and vice versa.
- *Suspicious/secretive*: the more one person closely examines another, the more that person takes refuges in concealment and vice versa.
- *Permissive/controlling or protector/enforcer* (regarding children): the more one person emphases unconditional love, the more the other emphasizes accountability or vice versa.

In all of these apparent deadlocks, two or more people become locked in roles that grow more rigid the more the other resists. A systems thinker may say that each person is a voice for an important value – each of which is needed by the other person.

Common Factors in Most Models of Systems Therapy

Sprenkle et al. (2009) have asserted that, regardless of their model, most couple and family therapists have these three factors in common:

- *They slow the process down.* If a non-judgemental therapist is able to listen and accept whatever trouble a family or couple bring into the office, other family members may also find permission to listen as well without losing their dignity.
- *They encourage clients to 'stand meta' to their situations.* This means to step out of their own point of view by modelling the understanding of the process as a whole pattern, rather than as the effect of one or more person's blameworthy behaviour. A systems therapist attempts to understand not only each person's feelings and perspective, but also the pattern between people that is the source of distress. Naming a frustrating cycle that causes couple or family distress can invite client reflection outside their own emotional point of view. When clients correct or add to the therapist's description, they become engaged in the process of themselves finding out the common source of their loved ones and their distress.
- *They encourage individual responsibility.* Each approach to therapy has its own path to motivating clients to think and act with more responsibility. How clients become more responsible without feeling judged or coerced is the art of therapy. For example, in couple therapy, Susan Johnson invites empathy for one's partner's unmet needs. In family therapy with adolescents, Ron Taffel makes a point of schooling teenagers about the effects of their behaviour on themselves and others. It is Rogers' theory, of course, that when understood and accepted exactly as they are, clients move in a more constructive direction.

A person-centred systems therapist changes a system by not being the same as the system, while accepting the system and seeking to understand it from the inside out. To 'slow down' a system's process, curiosity is privileged, as is empathic guessing that includes not only attention to each person's inner frame of reference but also the way in which their story interacts with other stories to give a richer, more complete picture. The therapist may say, 'Wait a minute, let me see if I understand you correctly' and, to others, 'What do you understand about what she is saying?'

Regarding 'standing meta', therapists look for patterns in clients' lives, but do not assume that they are accurate in their perception and descriptions. They demonstrate intent to understand rather than making a claim to understand. At the heart of the person-centred approach is the thought that no person's experience is the same as it may seem from the outside. The therapist who explains a pattern at the expense of listening to each person's experience creates exactly the know-it-all therapist that Rogers' innovation was able to bypass. In place of this knowing-all-about-it position is confident humility in dialogue. The therapist models looking for a new understanding of the situation in which the clients participate and of which they eventually take charge. Many patterns seen by clients emerge in paying close attention to in-the-roomtransactions. Sometimes, homework that includes filling out a genogram adds richness and complexity to clients' awareness.

'Individual responsibility' in a person-centred approach is more the result of clients freed from blame or coercion becoming more open to action than that of therapist pep talk. As we have seen in Chapter 2, clients are encouraged by their loved ones noticing their attempts to do something different. Recently, I have been asking some clients to write two notes on a piece of paper: the first note is 'advice' to the other client(s) in the room; the second is 'advice for themselves'. I never, of course, make this suggestion when hostility and mistrust are dominant. Frequently, the advice for the other is thoughtful and non-accusatory; the advice for self is insightful and useful. In general, individual responsibility is increased by clients' participation in discussion of the trouble that all members of the group have in common.

A person-centred systems therapist joins a couple and family in a search for lost wholeness, for overlooked intentions and frustrated hopes. I have sometimes described my work as the 'discovery business', in that I am looking for what is overlooked, trying to emerge healthy and health producing. Therapy can result in encouraging a family to look for their lost admiration (Gottman 1999), their forgotten successful organization and their under-estimated powers to perceive, connect and work together. The therapist can observe unexpected or overlooked differences in a family or couple's words or actions. It is not only the positive that the therapist notices. In fact, if they take a too earnest position of pointing out the positive, they can become like a naïve family member trying to talk people into getting along. It can be as important to state the losses and bleak choices facing people in a system so that they can experience being seen and accepted in their dilemmas.

My most persistent experience is that a change in a system takes place when one person commits to change *and* budgets for the long time it takes for any other person, first, to notice the existence of the change and, second. to begin to change themselves.

Active Facilitation of the Process

Unlike in work with individuals, the therapist has to commit to an active facilitation of the process. They have to ask each person to accept the commitment to dialogue that must mean listening as well as talking; agreeing to clarify; allowing time for translation by the therapist; and, perhaps most importantly, agree to the assumption that each person present has a different experience and has the right to express that experience without making another person wrong or invalid. Without this activity, the system prevents dialogue and discovery. Richard Stuart (1980) is perhaps one of the few couple therapists to formalize expectations of clients in writing before the therapy begins. Change in a family or couple eventually requires client reflection and listening rather than simply reacting to one another. Client reflection and listening become possible when they feel heard, understood and not under threat.

Family therapy, particularly, is about allowing people to be themselves and to say what is true for them without being entitled to have their loved ones agree with them or give them what they want. It is about trading in the fantasy of fulfilment of your wishes in the outer world for increased freedom in the inner world. Regarding couples, John Gottman has said it very well: every couple has at least one and usually more than one area of significant disagreement (Gottman and Silver 1999). Happier couples manage to treat each other with respect, kindness and a sense of humour when dealing with these difficulties.

A new awareness of one another as well as the way they work as part of a system along with a new awareness of one's own possibilities: that is the goal of couple and family therapy. Being able to be oneself without feeling that by so doing one is harming or being unfair to a loved one: that is the goal of couple and family therapy. Replacing a blame- and withdrawal-oriented pattern with an open system of expression and understanding: that is also the goal of couple and family therapy. The de-escalation of conflict and rejection and their replacement with an understanding of shared dilemmas and personal responsibility: that is the goal of relationship therapy.

Looking at Families of Origin

Intergenerational therapies attempt to meet these goals by explorations of the extended family field out of which a couple or nuclear family has formed itself. Box 3.2 offers a glimpse of the perspectives and tools that these models may offer.

Box 3.2: Intergenerational Therapies

There are many forms of intergenerational therapy, each of which can inform a person in work with families, couples and individuals. Family systems therapy or Bowen therapy (Bowen 1978; Friedman 1991) offers one rich way for any thera-pist to look at how a person can be influenced by the social system in which they grew up. This approach has many parallels with Carl Rogers' concept of 'condi-tions of worth' (Rogers 1959); that is, that a person may be out of touch with their own thoughts and feelings because they are living out family members' expectations. Bowen therapy often takes the form of prepared-for visits, one on one, with parents or siblings or even aunts, uncles and cousins, in order to perceive established family patterns more objectively and therefore liberate oneself from values introjected (Barrett-Lennard 1998) in childhood that are incongruent in one's present. A related approach is family of origin therapy, developed by James Framo (1992), in which adults, after several individual ther-apy sessions, meet with parents and/or siblings in at least two meetings spread over more than one day.

In my practice, parents may ask me to facilitate meetings with their adult children or adult children may ask for meetings with their parents. In each approach, clients are encouraged to:

- not attempt to change other family members;
- use 'I' statements that avoid characterizing or blaming others;
- practise listening skills and try to understand the other person's frame of reference;
- attempt to 'think meta' – that is, attempt to see the whole pattern of their family's way of being rather than their own needs or interpretations;
- see the ways in which they are pulled into certain roles and emotional states by family dynamics and explore ways to be less emotionally controlled and exer-cise more internal and external freedom.

Each reader may explore how important their own families of origin are in their current inner and outer lives. How are your current relationships similar to those of significant family members? What situations with partner or children produce strong emotional reactions out of proportion to their apparent significance? What person in your family bothers you the most, seems 'impossible' or makes you feel like a child? What have you tried to do about this? The person-centred therapist does not impose these or a hundred other questions on clients, but may be open to exploring such topics for them.

See O'Leary (1999) for an account of Carl Rogers' process of differentiation from his own family or origin as well as Rogers' (1961) description of the way a change in one woman led to change in both her mother and her daughter. See McGoldrick and Carter (2001) for an excellent discussion of re-evaluation of one's identity through encounters with significant family members. As in a person-centred approach, these therapists recommend conversations with members of one's family of origin in which the initiator is empathic and accepting rather than argumentative and judging.

Sometimes it may be helpful for a therapist to offer the following tools in relation to client need:

- *The genogram or family tree* (McGoldrick and Gerson 1985). For couples I see longer than briefly, I often give them a form to fill out showing all the people in each of their families at least as far back as their grandparents and aunts and uncles. At a glance one learns a great deal about family history, such as immigration, tragedy, losses, styles of relating to children, trauma. After the name of each person, short descriptions are used and relationships are described between significant people: How would you characterize your parents' relationship? Your grandparents'? What, in general, was expected of men in your family? Of women? There is an example of a genogram in Figure 3.1.
- *Couples filling out a genogram at home.* Each member of a couple filling out their family tree and discussing it at home serves several purposes. It allows a couple to 'stand meta' in relation to their issues, seeing them as part of a wider story of people relating to each other and their children over generations. It can also function as an opportunity to engage together seriously without getting caught up in the divisive issues that brought them into therapy. The therapist and clients may talk about what topics can be discussed at home without spilling into acrimony. Sometimes, another person's family of origin can itself be the central problem and the object of insulting, accusatory discourse.
- *Differentiating a family's way of being from the dominant story of their family of origin.* Each family both replicates *and* achieves an alternative to the patterns of the family with which each client grows up. A therapist's questions can encourage clients to notice ways in which they have chosen their own more functional paths. For instance, 'How is that you manage not to have the constant fighting you

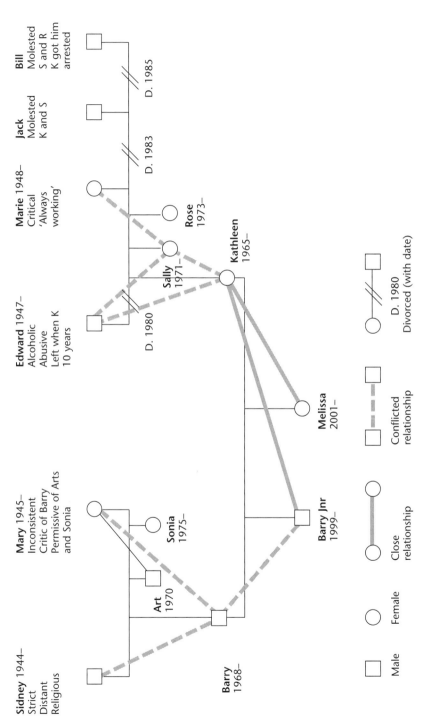

Figure 3.1 Example Genogram – Barry and Kathleen

describe from your childhood?' 'When did you know you would be able to treat your children differently from how you were treated?' 'What is it like for you to have children who expect you to listen and treat them with respect?' 'How did you manage to survive this childhood with a sense of optimism and confidence in your own abilities?' 'What is possible for you, now that you know your father was wrong about your ability to handle difficulty?'

The brief genogram in Figure 3.1, which includes only the parents and aunts and uncles of the family in therapy, revealed elements that helped Barry and Kathleen, whom we met in Case Example 2.1 in Chapter 2, recognize the systems pressures that influenced their fighting and impasses. As the oldest of two sisters who were molested and abused by two stepfathers, Kathleen emerged from her childhood as a fierce protector of victimized children. Although Barry was quite different from her father and stepfathers, his anger and, to her, difficulty with self-control made it difficult to trust him to work things out with her children. Barry, who had been abused and blamed by his parents and treated less well than his, in his eyes, less deserving siblings, absorbed some of his parents' punishing ways, especially at the thought that his children were 'getting away' with something. Though Barry and Kathleen, both oldest children, had emerged from childhood as effective survivors who managed a loving, respectful relationship with one another, frustration and tiredness would bring out a repeating conflict. Barry would enact his parents' punitive style when he thought that his kids were misbehaving. He could see Kathleen as like his parents: harsh to him, foolishly indulgent to his children (like his siblings). If Kathleen interfered, he would get angrier and more frustrated, rather than regain his composure as he would if left alone. (In fact, he was often an effective, understanding parent.) Kathleen, usually empathic and supportive of her husband, could become harsh and demanding towards him whenever she heard his voice raised.

Intellectual interpretations, especially from a therapist, may confuse issues and make clients passive. A person-centred approach privileges in-the-moment experiences over talking about the past. Awareness of past emotional pressures, however, may widen clients' understanding of their own feelings. A genogram in which clients make their own observations of the dynamics of a recurring problem can give them more options as well as more compassion for the pressures felt by their seeming adversary. I offer genograms in response to client requests for homework along with other tools. The longer a therapy continues, the more useful they become.

Dealing with Emotional Reactivity in Systems Therapy

Couple and family therapy is a vigorous meeting requiring a therapist whom clients see as empathic and powerful enough to facilitate a dialogue that is brave and true while being safe. It means offering enough safety for people to be able to tolerate listening to the versions of stories of people they at least used to love, somewhat depend on and now are at odds with. Safety, in this context, means the ability to translate sometimes very raw feelings into conversation. One student, asked what she needed in a family therapist, said: 'Someone larger than my father who could make space for him to listen to me.' She was talking both literally (her father was a large and powerful man) and metaphorically (she needed a therapist who could create safety to speak in the presence of a man she found intimidating). A person-centred therapist offers permission to each family member to change their perspective without losing their dignity or their freedom to choose.

Sometimes, in at least my career, the dialogue feels neither brave nor true. In the middle of a stormy or stagnant relationship, a meeting can feel ill advised and the therapist foolish. Milan group family psychiatrist Gianfranco Cecchin (1987) has written that sometimes a therapist may wish they had become a plumber or a waitress! The therapist must consistently deal with the magnetic pull of strong family negative emotions. Cecchin suggests the path of active curiosity rather than attempts to control or fix. The therapist uses their position and powers to pay attention to clients' feelings and intentions rather than accusations and claims of superiority. Neurology and temperament are part of the system that all participants in therapy must learn to manage. Humans get 'hi-jacked by the amygdala, that is: fall under the control of the instinctual part of the brain that counsels "fight or flight."' (Wylie 2004). Clients and therapists alike can go in and out of emotional states that keep them from making contact in the present.

Systems therapy requires becoming aware of emotional reactivity as opposed to genuine emotion. The first is a defence of self-concept in the face of perceived threat and brings unhelpful fear and/or aggression into a situation. The second can be the expression of primary emotion without externally oriented blame or attack that often has the effect of clarifying and simplifying relationships; it can be called 'softening' language (Johnson and Greenberg 1994), which invites collaboration and support rather than defensiveness and avoidance. The systems thinker privileges the understanding of the immediate conversation between people rather than the untangling of confusing power struggles. For example, following a father's harsh words to a teenaged son, I said: 'So right now you are very angry and it's like you almost don't mind if you hurt your son. Is that right? You are so angry you don't even mind what effect your words have? Would you say that you are not just angry right now but hostile?' The banal intellectual distinction between anger and hostility is one that had been discussed in calmer times. I am asking for the father's attention away from his monologue and into engagement with our work in therapy and, temporarily, with me. He will either agree with me or be annoyed at my pomposity. In any event, he is invited into a working mode rather than his ranting mode.

When clients are in their fighting, aggressive systems, I ask them to look at me when they speak rather than at each other. When they look at one another they can be drawn into the electrical system of an intense competition, 'an absorbing state' (Johnson and Greenberg 1994). When they look at me they allow us to be in psychological contact; I am willing to accept them and listen to what they say. I then look at the other person and offer a translation that the other person can listen to with less agitation.

JANE: *(To me)* He may as well admit he doesn't love me. He is cold as ice. Completely self-centred.

THERAPIST: *(To Bill)* I am lonely. I am hurt because you don't seem to care about me any more. *(To Jane)* Did I get this right?

BILL: *(To me)* You have completely turned into a different person. You start yelling at me the minute I come into the house. I never have a moment's peace.

THERAPIST: *(To Jane)* You are not the same to me as you used to be. It's hard for me to talk with you when you are angry. *(To Bill)* Did I get that right?

What follows are descriptions of family or couple therapy at the beginning, in the middle and near the end. In systems therapy all sessions contain a focus on experiences in the room: clients' dialogue – directly addressing each other; sharing feelings, thoughts, needs, wishes and difficulties; experimenting with different ways of communicating. There is also an element of shared curiosity: What are the elements in the present wider circle that are commonly experienced threats, challenges and opportunities? How are today's difficulties related to past troubles as well as successes? How is this family doing in their meeting of their life circumstances compared to generations preceding them? The therapy slows communication down so that each may feel heard and listen; the therapy is an opportunity for getting a wider lens perspective of their current trouble; finally, the therapy provides an opportunity for each person both to change and to take note of others' attempts to change.

Person-Centred Systems Therapy at the Beginning

In early sessions, a couple and family therapist is establishing a relationship with clients while facilitating a definition of their issues that reflects their goals. The therapist balances openness to the clients' points of view with offering choices about how to shape the process of the therapy.

I chose Case Example 3.1 because it illustrates the importance of a systems point of view – in this instance, not assuming that Carolyn's feelings would stay the same if her experience of Gene changed even a little.

Case 3.1: The Risk of Inviting Your Partner into Therapy

Carolyn, a former client who, along with her husband Gene, had met with this therapist ten years before because of a work-related crisis at Gene's job, asked to see him individually. She wanted to get over her anger at Gene and 'just accept the fact they were living almost separate lives or, on the other hand, decide the marriage was over and pursue separation'.

The therapist listened to her as she told her story. As best he could, he tuned into her feelings, allowing her to risk describing some of the aloneness and frustration she was experiencing. She shared her dilemma: loving Gene, not thinking he loved her. She was comfortable being married to Gene and did not know what life would be like without him. She also knew that she couldn't go on with this much coldness and distance between them. She particularly disliked his intense involvement in a highly successful competitive bowling team that seemed to her to be a rival, almost another partner, which he 'clearly' preferred to her. She 'couldn't win': if she was silent, she felt cowardly and used and left for someone else; if she complained, she felt stuck either with his promising to have less to do with the team without changing at all, with a defence of his behaviour or with him missing team events in such a sullen manner that she didn't want him around.

The therapist had no need to contradict any of her assertions. Why wouldn't they be true? He was, however, able to be aware of other realities co-existing with her story. What had happened to their rela-tionship before Gene's increasingly intense relationship with the team? What would Gene say about how Carolyn acted when she was with him? Did he feel loved, attended to, understood? Did he perceive Carolyn as having a rival interest? What would it take to change the nature of the conversations they had about the bowling team? What other factors – at work, in their families of origin, in their health, in their intimate contact – were influencing their life together? These kinds of questions, similar to the Milan group's 'circular questions' (Boscolo et al. 1987), are a way of systems thinking that sometimes is spoken, sometimes remains in the background.

The therapist let these questions emerge in their conversation. Carolyn was able to reflect on them even while she felt free to vent her frustration without the therapist correcting her perceptions. The indi-vidual therapy evolved towards the question: Why not invite Gene into the sessions? The therapist did not in any way insist that the therapy become a couple's meeting. Carolyn would be taking a risk in two ways: Gene could refuse to come and she would be left feeling even more rejected than before; if he did come in, the therapy would bring their situation to a more explicit crisis that could conceivably make matters worse. Continuing to see a therapist individually, however, could strengthen the assumption that her marriage was a finished book rather than a volume with unfinished chapters. In the earliest sessions, clients make decisions that shape the future process of the relationship. A therapist's confidence and openness to couple and family dialogue can help clients reawaken dormant dialogue.

Carolyn did decide to invite Gene into the sessions and he readily agreed to come. The therapy brought the struggle between their rela-tionship and his bowling team into clear focus. More importantly, the many reasons each had for gradually feeling unloved and criticized and their increased unspoken questions and disappointments had a safe place for expression.

Early sessions can have these elements:

- Empathy for each individual.
- A distinction between the situation they find themselves in and what they had intended when they first got together and what they want now; a description of 'the It' (Jacobson) or the externalized problem that blamed no one.

- Compassion about the situation rather than assignment of blame for one or the other.
- Gradual information gathering about who they are; how long they have been together; previous relationships; children and pleasures and difficulties with those children; money issues; work issues. Some of this is gathered by paperwork each fills out and some is gathered in an 'oh by the way' manner as they tell stories and discuss problems. Clients answering written questions can, without interrupting dialogue, can provide information that a therapist can and should know, like number of children in families of origin; previous relationships; whose children are whose; major events, recent or past, that may continue to have an impact.
- Explanatory statements about what they can expect, e.g. This is what I will be doing:trying to listen for what each of you is frustrated about. I will also be doing this: finding out what parts of your relationship are just fine. As you can see, I will be trying to find out what it is like for each of you. I appreciate that you understand that part of this work is that you listen to the other, even though you don't agree at all, knowing that I will give you each of you a chance to put your side of things.
- A request for some statement of what their relationship is like when it is good. Usually I end with this, so that the session becomes not just about the current distress but also about the reason the couple would commit to this difficult dialogue as well as a vision of them as expert in the session. For example. the most important expertise is when they are able to be in harmony and congruent while at the same time accepting the other.

Most of these are systems interventions. Early sessions invite people to have a systems perspective about their troubles.

Person-Centred Therapy in the Middle

In the middle of therapy, clients assume more ownership of the therapy and the ability to talk about important emotional issues with less accusation and more confidence in being heard. Clients identify the effect they have on others, along with the effect others have on them. Having had some experience of successful communication during and between sessions, they are able to take risks in self-expression, knowing that their listeners are better able to hear challenging thoughts without immediately feeling rejected. Difficult conversations are attempted and work on core issues becomes possible.

Case Example 3.2: Peg and Ralph Learn to Communicate in a New Reality

Peg and Ralph were in crisis after the failure of Rob's two bookstores. The first, highly successful, was brought down by the closure of the second, begun because of Ralph's insistence that it was a safe investment. The couple not only became bankrupt, but also lost a significant amount of money that had been invested by Peg's brother. The couple were defeated, discouraged and unable to spend money on recreation or even very good food. Between them was an unbearable subject: Ralph had let them down, however unintentionally, and felt like a failure; Peg was holding them together financially, though Ralph had found jobs well beneath his former income level. The couple had a strong commitment to each other, loved each other and were grieving not only for their lost security and financial status, but also for their sense of pride, optimism and equality.

In early sessions the couple worked on Peg's ability to express her frustration, not with the past event but with Ralph's, to her, defeated attitude and unwillingness to seek a new way of being successful. She also wanted him to resume talking with her brother and working to restore the harmony of her family. Ralph, in his turn, felt that Peg treated him like a second-class citizen, was in absolute charge of the money in the family, seemed to criticize him and their kids too freely and had not really ever forgiven him for their losses. Early therapy was characterized by allowing each to speak and then hear how the other received what they said. 'Follow advocacy with inquiry' is a rule in business facilitation that applies also to family systems (Schwartz 2002); another rule that is a sign of good process in therapy is 'discuss all undiscussible issues' without flooding the other with blame or hopelessness.

The couple saw their therapist every two weeks. Clients who stay past the beginning of therapy can gradually take charge of its direction and become more comfortable with honest give and take. Ralph was able to tell Peg how he felt about the rules regarding money in the home and her unspoken sense of being his victim. Sessions spent sharing family-of-origin experiences allowed each person to understand more about the other's expectations of life, hopes and vulnerabilities.

He could let her know that her expectation that 'he find a new goal and pursue it' seemed patronizing to him and did not respond to his sense that at mid-life his dream business had turned to ashes and that he could not picture any work in the future that would excite or even interest him. The couple began to experience what narrative therapist Michael White calls unique outcomes (White and Epson 1990) or moments when things go unexpectedly well: they could put aside their usual pattern and experience a fuller connection than might have been expected. Peg was able to express genuine sadness about Ralph's loss of his joyful life's work without having her own sense of victimization take centre stage. Peg's genuine response to his feelings made Ralph feel more dignified and like a man cared about by his wife, rather than the guy who had ruined her life. Freed from that image, Ralph became more active on his own behalf, taking more initiatives with regard to household tasks. He was also able to talk about considerations of future work possibilities. Peg reported that Ralph had taken initiatives to have more contact with her brother.

The middle of therapy is not always pleasant or easy. For each connection made, the clients can make false attempts at respectful, caring conversations that can end in hurt or being 'back where we started'. It is characteristic of the middle of therapy that couples make more corrections of their divisive, blaming or confusing conversations and show greater ability to respond to the deeper requests behind their family members' words.

Mid-therapy sessions may have these elements:

- Empathy for each person as they react to the change unfolding in the system.
- Unexpected change, for the worse as well as the better, in a person's self-concept as another person's change affects their role and tasks.
- Sharing of early relationship experiences, good and bad, and family-of-origin conditions that influence emotional and intellectual ways of dealing with a predicament.
- Clients ask for and do homework such as genograms and communication exercises that they think fit their particular needs.
- Increased possibilities of family or couple members describing issues with a wider lens than their own particular frame of reference. This wider vision of issues can come and go. Individuals can regress in

crisis to a static, self-centred view of a situation, then feel relief if they are able to see the context of the issue.

- Increased relaxation, freedom, commentary on the process, more seeing themselves as others see them. Family psychiatrist Frank Pittman, author of *Grow Up!* (1998), has commented that at the beginning of therapy people talk about how they feel and what others do to them and gradually learn more about how others feel and how they affect others.
- Usually a crisis occurs in which the old ways of seeing self and others prevail, followed by the application of one or more learnings from the therapy.

Person-Centred Therapy near the Ending

It is characteristic of a successful ending of therapy that clients accept more of the other person(s) positions while making, at least, partial attempts to change their own. Often, some initiative takes place that signals greater ability to handle the predicaments that brought the clients to therapy.

Case Example 3.3: Dee and Mark – a Transition for a Mother and Son

A recently single parent, Dee, came to therapy with her oldest son Mark, who was 17. Mark, very bright, was under-performing in school and, though polite and clearly loving his mother, no longer felt a need to follow her rules at home. Mark was in love, very sexually active and very attentive to his girlfriend, who lived alternately with her two divorced parents, both of whom complained vigorously that she should live with the other and not give them so much trouble. His girlfriend, Jenni, was often sick with unclear gastrointestinal symptoms that sometimes gave her so much pain that she needed lifts to hospital emergency departments, which, since neither of her parents was willing to provide them, became Mark's responsibility, whatever the hour, whatever his other obligations.

This mother and son, who had enjoyed a close, loving relationship, were divided by their own sense of obligation and integrity. Dee wanted to be a good mother who shepherded her son through his last year of secondary school and into university; she was very afraid of his getting entangled with a young woman who came from a much less supportive environment than her son and who had far less to lose (in her own eyes) if she became pregnant or if Mark failed school because of his attention to her.

Mark, on the other hand, considered himself an adult with his own responsibilities. His first obligation now was not to his mother but to the girl he loved. If he was unable to finish school or go to university or please his parents, that was the way it had to be.

What was most important, to the therapist, was that each person showed up for the therapy hoping for what only Dee could articulate. Could there be some path in which each could be true to themselves while resolving their state of war?

The therapist facilitated a series of conversations that allowed each to say what they valued and saw as important. Multi-directional partiality was most important throughout this therapy; each person not only made sense to themselves but also felt deserving respect for their values. Each needed to learn the other's point of view without losing their right not to agree to it. The therapist highlighted each person's sense of obligation: Dee *had* to make sure that her son was allowed to be young and a student for a while longer; Mark *had* to be true to his girlfriend and his obligation to be there for her regardless of cost.

It was also important to bring up some of the unspoken issues that existed in the field. Mark had not told Dee about all his feelings regarding the divorce his father had initiated two years before. Dee had not told Mark of her sadness that his father's life seemed to have become harder and less predictable after the divorce. Mark was not immune to worry about the consequences of teenage fatherhood before he had even learned to hold down a full-time job; he also had some feelings of sadness at how impossible his life had become being a sleepy student by day and a rescuer by night. Dee had sadness about the way in which Jenni seemed to have no one there for her and no reason not to dream that a new baby would bring resolution to her problems. Jenni attended one of the sessions at Mark's request.

Near the end of the therapy, Mark believed that perhaps Jenni was pregnant. Neither of her parents was interested in getting her medical attention. (This is a frequent issue with teenagers: their friends may be left to their own devices by parents less caring than their own. They are pulled to fill a vacuum of caring before they are established in their own lives.) The therapist asked if Dee had considered bringing some of her attention to this young girl in distress. Dee decided outside the session that she would initiate a visit for Jenni to her own gynaecologist and accompanied her to the visit. Jenni was not pregnant and the doctor initiated a more reliable birth control method. Dee's adult caring freed Mark of premature responsibility. Relationship therapy finishes successfully when clients take initiatives that favour their own sense of responsibility rather than attempted control of the other. Dee found a path to a wider definition of motherhood.

In the final session of therapy, Mark and Dee talked more about Mark's school and what it would take for him to go to university next year. They discussed some of the logistics of Mark's coming and going between parents in his unreliable car. He saw less of Jenni than he did at the beginning of the therapy. The therapist did not see them again for another year, until they came in to work on including Dee's suddenly orphaned 16-year-old nephew in their household.

The therapy ended with this mother and son finding a different way for her to remain a mother and him still to be a son in need of support. Systems thinking allowed for both/and in conceptualizing the issues and facilitating conversation. No one had to be wrong, but all relevant topics, including fears and unspoken needs, could be brought up. Dialogue allowed for more creative actions outside the therapy.

Sessions at the end of therapy can have these elements:

- An established pattern of each person having a voice without the other having to be wrong.
- Inclusion of other people, issues and developmental needs in the dialogue.
- Awareness that change will come less by asserting control over the other than by caring action.
- Attempts at 'switched vigilance' (Abrams-Spring 2007), in which one person pays attention to meeting a need of the other that was formerly a source of contention and frustration – and, optimally, vice versa.
- The use of the therapy session for whatever conversation either wants to initiate.
- The establishment of a dialogue in which roles (e.g. mother/son) are acknowledged but also allowed to change in nature.

Conclusion

Systems thinking offers unique responsibilities in the practice of Rogers' six therapeutic conditions. In connecting to individuals, showing them acceptance and understanding their points of view, the therapist must show multi-directional partiality or willingness to be on each person's side without rejecting the points of view and interests of the other people present. The therapist attempts to acknowledge each person's need without denying other perspectives. Each therapist shows interest not only in the current reality seen by the clients, but in their preferred future realities and their lost, mourned-for past opportunities and expectations. The good systems therapist does not deny clients' description of their situation, but is also curious about other unspoken awareness and unnoticed resources.

Rogers' six conditions are all relevant here, as will be shown in the next chapter as well as Chapter 5, but most important may be the third condition (The therapist is congruent), because a non-anxious person without a hidden agenda has an immediate calming effect on clients that allows them to begin to see their situation and meet it more consciously.

4

The Core Conditions of the Person-Centred Approach

Reliance on the clients' own resources, revived and sustained by relationship, is the heart not only of a person-centred approach, but of the collaborative approaches described in Chapter 1. Can I be there for the clients so that they are encouraged to be there for themselves? Consistent with meta-research on successful therapy that emphasizes the importance of the therapeutic relationship (Asay and Lambert 1999; Cooper 2008), this chapter will offer a couple and family therapist's perspective on Rogers' six necessary and sufficient conditions for therapeutic change:

1. Two persons are in psychological contact.
2. The first, whom we shall term the client, is in a state of incongruence, being vulnerable or anxious.
3. The second person, whom we shall term the therapist, is congruent or integrated in the relationship.
4. The therapist experiences unconditional positive regard for the client.
5. The therapist experiences an empathic understanding of the client's internal frame of reference and endeavours to communicate this experience to the client.
6. The communication to the client of the therapist's empathic understanding and unconditional positive regard is to a minimal degree achieved.

Reflection on these conditions will deepen awareness of the practices relevant to relationship therapy presented in Chapter 2 and offer more examples of therapist experience and behaviour.

The Necessary Therapeutic Conditions in the Relationship Therapy Context

Conducting or supervising research on individual therapy sessions for over 20 years, Carl Rogers gradually worked towards a bold formulation of elements necessary and sufficient for therapeutic change. These conditions, the subject of dozens of studies, have been much described in a wide-ranging literature (see Barrett-Lennard 1998, 2005 and Cooper 2008 for discussion and research findings). These six conditions, the heart of person-centred practice, can serve as a reliable source of support for the couple and family therapist. The therapist, looking at the outcome of a past session or preparing for the next, can locate trouble and opportunity by considering the conditions listed below. For example, a seemingly satisfied couple who make a second appointment but don't keep it or return a follow-up call may well have found something missing in the therapeutic process. A therapist may examine whether empathy was displaced by eagerness to share an idea or insist on a reframe that was opposed or, worse, irrelevant to the client. Perhaps a brief written evaluation (Burns 2010) may have revealed clients' disappointment in the therapist's ability to understand, accept and show responsiveness to clients' goals.

1. Two persons are in psychological contact

In relationship therapy, therapists are there for each individual whom they greet and invite into participation. Susan Johnson, co-founder of the client-centred emotion focused couple therapy, writes of re-engaging the more detached members (2004). Some clients are quiet and content to be on the sidelines; some are withdrawn because other family members are seen as critical or even to dislike them. Therapists make explicit permission not to talk even while they are interested in what might keep a client from active participation. The therapist is committed to help each person find a way to be part of a therapy seen as useful to them.

Rogers (1957) said: 'All that is intended in this first condition is to specify that the two (or more) people are to some degree in contact, that each makes a difference in the experiential field of the other.' Therapists must not be attached to the cherished ways in which they would want their own therapists to make contact. For many male clients especially, therapist silence is *not* golden but a sign of bafflement, detachment or weakness. Conversation that is responsive, that explains and that makes sense of the reason for meeting, may be necessary until the clients feel comfortable enough to take charge of the meeting.

Master therapist for families of adolescents Ron Taffel (2005) connects with young people because of his knowledge of their music, and the meaning of the clothes and other decorations they wear or have had mechanically made part of them. He knows television shows that kids are likely to watch as well as movies. The therapist does not have to like these things – in fact, over-eagerness to be cool is, of course, uncool – but he may have to like or be relaxed about the clients liking them. School family therapist (a newly created position in a New York school district) Dave Seaburn (2007) has said that whether his students come for more than one therapy session depends on 'liking'. Not that he likes them – that must be taken for granted – but that 'they like me!' meaning, perhaps, that young people experience his interest and acceptance.

To make contact, I usually listen, find out and follow up what is said with empathic conjecture. To make contact, I sometimes talk, briefly, and in the service of clients talking. I weave a commentary so that new clients and old clients are supported and encouraged to try new things. Here are some of descriptive statements and questions I might offer:

- 'You are listening in as your wife talks about something she is very angry about. You are sitting there concentrating on her. What would you like her to know you are thinking?'
- 'Would I be right to say that this is one of the most important things you really want us to understand about you?'
- 'It looks like your partner is asking if you have noticed the way he has been trying to change. Can you respond to him now or do you need room to say something else?'
- 'Here you are. You two used to share similar opinions, but now it is important for you to let her know how different from her you have become.'
- 'You can love him as he becomes more expressive of his own way, but it is hard not to let him know that you miss the old way you two used to talk.'
- 'It looks like your mother would really like you to say something right now. Is there anything you are able to say or do you not feel ready to speak?'
- 'I have heard many women say the men in their lives "just don't get it". Can you say right now what you do think you understand about her?'

● 'How did she do just now? Is that closer?' (This statement is less inviting a judgment than opening the door to the kind of reflection that makes change possible.)

Psychological contact is never a given: clients indicate to an observant therapist when they feel engaged and when they feel shut down and that changes from session to session. Change in contact can relate to changes in clients or to their reaction to signals that the therapist's acceptance has become more conditional or the therapist's opinions more central. In a flourishing therapy each person is welcomed and feels co-ownership of the therapy hour. One family I met with, full of school children half in primary, half in secondary schools, had everyone raising their hands for their chance to talk. Contact with each person means willingness to adapt to the conversation on their terms.

Case Example 4.1: Connecting with Clare

For example, when in a first session Clare talks about her anger at her husband Tom's apparent indifference to her feelings, the therapist referred to the wider difficulty that research shows American men to have in showing emotional support for American women (Gottman 1999). Clare says quickly that this is much worse than the usual male/female trouble and that we will be wasting our time if we look at it that way. I revert, as I should have from the beginning, to reflecting back accurately what she is saying.

THERAPIST: You want it understood that this is more than usual male/female trouble. The stakes are higher: you want me and Tom to know that we won't get anywhere unless we take this trouble very seriously.

CLARE: Yes, and I don't think he will be able to do it. He always starts off that he's going to really change this time, but then if things get a little better, he's right back to his own self.

THERAPIST: You really have doubts that this will be any different than it has been in the past. Yet you came here.

CLARE: Well, I love him. But I'm not going to keep working on this the way I have all these years. He's going to have to change without me making it easy for him.

THERAPIST: You're going to come to the therapy, but you want it known that he'll have to change because he wants to, not because you are pushing him.

> CLARE: I'm not going to come. He's going to have to come and start changing. Then I'll see.
>
> The therapist could not meet this client unless he was willing to suspend expectations of her, whether or not she came to therapy.
>   The therapist, persistent and usually committed to reframe in first sessions, tried to make psychological contact by softening what Clare is saying. He could only *keep* contact with her by yielding to her insistence that her feelings be heard in full strength. Throughout the conversation she corrected his reflection until her position was fully recognized. She also facilitated connection with Tom by her admission: 'I love him.' Like many women deciding whether or not to stay in a long marriage, she expected Tom to do the work of changing in this part of their lives, but her expression of feelings for him brought hope into the process. In early stages, women are often seen as bearing responsibility for attention to the relationship (Gottman 1999).

Therapists are present to people first and to their model second. If children or teenagers are invited to the session, the therapist must adapt to their needs and their sense of being included. Belgian family therapist Peter Rober (2005) gives an example of an 8-year-old girl showing a picture to a therapist who, busy with gathering family history, told her that she would look at it later. The picture and the little girl's involvement were not offered again. The therapist's faithfulness to her own (seemingly reasonable) method was privileged over her responsiveness to the young client's way of entering the therapy. Making contact is always both/and: having a method for facilitating a meaningful dialogue *and* making way for clients' unique ways of being in the therapy hour. When I meet with children, I always have movement exercises, art materials and age-appropriate questions available *and* I yield to topics, ideas and requests that they bring in.

2. *The first, whom we shall term the client, is in a state of incongruence, being vulnerable or anxious*

Incongruence may be defined 'as a discrepancy between the actual experience of the organism and the self-picture of the individual's experience insofar as it represents that experience' (Rogers 1957: 222; Warner 2007:

155). It is a gap between what we think we are and what we think we should be. We are out of line with what we expect. Warner describes individual clients as experiencing a threat to their self-concept. She goes on to say, 'Perhaps in Condition 2, Rogers is simply saying that clients must … sense themselves as having issues that cause them problems or discomfort.' A whole family can be out of line with what they or one or more members think they should be; one or more individual members stumbling on their life journey or a persistent state of 'not being among friends' in one's own home creates the need for couple or family therapy.

In relationship therapy, loss of congruence is both the cause and the effect of increased anxiety and frustration. Members of families frequently see one another as untrustworthy, unfair and, especially, out of alignment with a formerly acceptable self. Clients can communicate in one-sided accusatory language at odds with their deeper desire for connection. They also experience themselves as no longer the effective or contented partner, child, sibling or friend they once were. They feel out of line with themselves and impossibly torn between blaming and rejecting their loved ones or collapsing in blame or rejection of themselves. 'Fine!' said a client about feedback she was getting from her husband. 'I will give him all the credit for everything and myself all the blame and go back to being a doormat!' Incongruence is alienation; it is being out on a limb; it is facing impossible choices.

Incongruence that is several generations in the making can arrive in the middle of a family. A woman may feel that she *must* be in charge of the raising of the children even while she marries a man with whom she discusses an equal share in all things regarding their offspring. She can be in great distress, exercising a need to control his behaviour with their children even while she resents how totally alone she feels in responsibility for the children. He can be defensive about his rights as a father even while he fails to attend to the hundred weekly tasks that go into their care. It sometimes takes a crisis over children, money or sex for people to realize that they are living a twenty-first-century life while feeling nineteenth-century feelings. A genogram (McGoldrick and Gerson 1985) or family tree, described in Chapter 3, can be a means of raising clients' curiosity about the roots of conflict.

Incongruence in couples and families can have these qualities:

- Inability to see other people as separate from their emotionally familiar roles. Much family and couple therapy arises from inevitable, individual change – e.g. a teenager exercising autonomy, a woman redefining 'wife' or 'mother' – being seen as a threat by others.

- Inability to see the discrepancy between a person's expected role and their in-the-moment capability. Early Rogers' collaborator Dick Farson (1987) has said, 'the combination of thinking a parent *should* know what to do and the fact they *don't* know what to do are the conditions for abuse'. (I have memorized this concept, which has been useful in countless predicaments throughout my career.)
- Insistence on credit to which you feel entitled in your own role while neglecting the requirements of that role, e.g. a father demanding respect while not paying close attention to the day-to-day emotions and needs of his child, or a mother focusing on her own hurt feelings and loneliness rather than her child's age-appropriate independence and separation.
- Awareness of your partner's withholding of time, attention, generosity, willingness to listen and support without consciousness of your own withdrawal of those same qualities.
- Expression of anger or resentment through raging tirades, sarcasm, unacknowledged 'paying back' or withdrawal rather than through direct communication.
- The habit of behaving in a sullen, resentful, unreasonable, unyielding, inauthentic way while assuming that you are fair, clear, assertive and open.
- Resenting your loved ones for changing despite the inevitable arrival of different ages, different conditions and different possibilities; or, conversely, resenting your loved one for *not* changing despite your earlier acceptance of them just as they were. For example, in the former condition a man may complain, 'You are not the woman I fell in love with.' In the latter, a woman may say, 'But you should have known I would change my mind about wanting children.'
- 'Pulling for' (Johnson and Greenberg 1994) the very words or behaviour you least want: 'Just admit it. In the end, sooner or later, you are going to leave me!'

Dan Wile has written elegantly, accurately and humorously about 'The Impossibility of Obeying the Rules of Good Communication' (1993: 249–265). *Incongruence is a natural process*; recognition of incongruence is the beginning of wisdom but not the end of relational complexity. It is important to note that humans can live relatively happily with incongruence that a therapist might notice if looking really hard. Many contented adults had parents who spoke for them, understood them poorly, formulated impossibly inaccurate theories about their character and tried to talk them into aspirations they did not want. The therapist does not act as a police officer, catching people at their incongruence, cleverly saying things like: 'You are smiling while you say you are angry.' The therapist's steady, 'non anxious presence' (Friedman 1991) allows clients to notice and create a process of recovery from incongruence insofar as it causes particular distress at particular times in their lives.

The therapist does not find villains or victims in couples and families. Carl Rogers saw clients as struggling to present themselves to themselves and others as better than they were (Kirschenbaum and Henderson 1990). If clients meet therapists who accept them wholly, they may be gradually allowed to let go of the need for incongruence.

3. *The second person, whom we shall term the therapist, is congruent or integrated in the relationship*

Carl Rogers stated his intention and goals as a therapist many times:

> Can I be in such a way which will be perceived by the other person as trustworthy, as dependable in some deep sense? … I have come to realize that being trustworthy does not demand that I be rigidly consistent but that I be dependably real. The term 'congruent' is one I have used to describe the way I would like to be. (Kirschenbaum and Henderson 1989, 1990: 108)

Attempting to understand the effect of Carl Rogers and his work, psychiatrist and author Peter Kramer (2002) remarked, 'Did he merely, as he claimed, accept the other or did he provide parts of his own differentiated self?' Psychotherapy researcher Germain Lietaer comments, 'Personal maturity, together with the basic therapeutic attitudes related to it can … be considered as the therapist's main instrument in client-centred therapy' (Lietaer 2001: 41 quoted in Cornelius-Whyte 2007). Rogers was consistent with clients, associations and friends alike. 'What he said to you early in the morning at his home was exactly what he would say later that day to a large group,' said his friend Alberto Zuconni (personal communication 2004). Much admired contemporary family therapist Michael White has been characterized as only talking about his clients as he would talk if they were present (Wylie 1994).

Congruence in the presence of families and couples is a foundation for all the relationship therapist's communication. Empathy or acceptance is of use only from a person who is seen as real and worthy of respect. The therapist manages to be present inside clients' relationships while maintaining their own sense of self and their own purpose in being there. In relationship therapy, alliance with one client against another – usually shown by benevolent attempts to convince that client of something they 'should' do or accept – or irritation with clients is best noticed first by the therapist than by the clients! The therapist can then decide to back up towards a clearer understanding of the temporarily least sympathetic client, rather than becoming stuck in 'harmful struggle' (Butler and Bird 2000). Commitment to congruence does not mean that you never lose balance and non-attachment, but that you take responsibility for managing your biases so that the other therapeutic conditions are not lost.

Throughout my career many selves have developed and some join my conversations, without my noticing it, and bring judgemental, authoritarian, impulsive or, unattractively, self-congratulatory elements to my therapy moments. For example:

- *Becoming unconscious of my own tendency to react out of judgement or fear or both.* For instance, 'I truly cannot understand why you would be mean when you know the effects it has on Jane.' I actually did say this, in innocent candour, to a male client who kept saying, 'I come home and I see myself being mean to her but I can't stop it.' Then I remembered my wife driving our car and my tone of voice: 'What are you doing? I can't believe this! Didn't you see that exit? Do you need me to drive?' and worse. Suddenly, I was a congruent man who knew that he could quite definitely be mean despite all his intentions and was able to go from judgement to empathy. It was important to share this with the client!
- *Feeling 'urgency, anxiety, over-responsibility and pessimism'* (Duncan et al. 1997a) and therefore creating an 'impossible' therapy. For me, over-responsibility opens the door to trying too hard to control clients, which leads to confusion for everyone. It is not that I don't have, can't own and can't express my own opinions, worries and convictions. It is that they must be congruent with my role as a therapist who is a real human being rather than an authority whose wishes must be obeyed.
- *Getting overwhelmed by the amount of inner and outer trouble in a couple or family and adding my own fear or anger to the family's stress.* At my worst, I can almost scold clients and add my own disapproval to an already very difficult situation. If I am congruent, I am able to notice my own arousal and do something to calm myself that may well

calm the family. For example, I may ask permission to tell what I see as the story as they present it. In a calm voice, I narrate what I have heard and seen in a chronology, with plenty of room for empathic expression of how people are showing that they feel. Any situation can be turned into a story. The telling of a story is a universal way to bring order to chaos. One person's story telling can invite other people's story telling and the calm of thoughtfulness can meet the distress of frustration and anxiety.

- *Becoming intoxicated by my own cleverness and goodness and at how well the therapy is going because of me.* Attention on the therapist is not the object of any useful therapy – certainly not on how he, and he alone, managed to help these people. How are the clients feeling? What is their sense of what is being learned? What does whatever happened, however apparently useful, mean to them? What do they now want to share with each other? Conversely, the therapist's feelings of inadequacy and fear should be acknowledged inwardly, but rarely shared any more than he shares his appreciation of his own personal charm. Good therapists attend to what the clients think, feel and need and trusts them, with sometimes strong support, to define what in their lives must be changed and what accepted.

The relationship therapist's ability to notice the coming and going of their own emotional reactivity brings their clients a model for how to behave with one another. Family members can be so absorbed in their own frame of reference, and especially their own urgent need to influence each other, that they can be unaware of their unintended impact.

4. The therapist experiences unconditional positive regard for the client

In successful relationship therapy, all clients feel that their position makes sense to the therapist. Clients who feel good about therapy experience ownership, safety and belonging. It is their therapy and they know that what they bring to it will matter and that they will leave as valued and important people. Condition 4 is the foundation of this experience and is needed at least as much in relationship therapy as in individual therapy. (In Chapter 7 we will see that finding ways to show acceptance in the form of noticing the positive is essential in the family therapy of families under great stress.) Clients do not want themselves or the relationship they bring with them to be the object of even subtle therapist disapproval. 'You don't judge us,' one client told a therapist to explain why they were continuing therapy despite many obstacles. Fortunately, she said this just before the therapist was about to give her and her partner some advice that he thought they needed! Truly unconditional positive regard was and continues to be a great innovation in therapy that needs to be learned again every session and privileged over the therapist's knowledge and experience.

In relationship therapy, of course, the therapist meets with two or more people whose claim to acceptance may be accompanied by a demand for the rejection or repudiation of the other people present. The therapist steadily occupies a place of respect and understanding of each person, despite any apparent paradox of doing so. The therapist relies on language that relies on the many dimensions of systems reality. For example, the therapist may say:

- 'Here you are in this dilemma. Each of you holds a core value that seems to meet an apparently opposite value in your partner. Does this make sense?'
- (The therapist stands up) 'Here is the side of parenting that you represent – what should we call it? The tough love side? Here is the side that you represent – would it be the support side? What else can we say about this side of the room? That side?' (Standing up and making the dilemma spatial or kinaesthetic gives people a chance to be observers of a whole process rather than defenders of one position and judges of another.)
- 'I am in the middle of the two of you: this feels awful. What's it like for each of you to be in this fight?' (This is a version of Neal Jacobson's concept of 'the It' (Jacobson and Christiansen 1996), the third element in the room that keeps a couple or a family from trusting and accepting one another.)
- (Also related to 'the It') 'It sounds hard for you to talk to each other easily when you each feel so defeated by this bankruptcy that almost seems to have taken over your marriage.'

Concepts originally articulated by Carl Rogers and his associates can be found in Neal Jacobson's more teaching-oriented behavioural couple therapy, as shown in Box 4.1.

Box 4.1: A Behavioural Couple Therapy Parallel

Active teaching and modelling of targeted skills form an, at least, 40-year-old tradition in behavioural couple therapy and integrated behavioural therapy (Atkins et al 2003). Some recent trends in behavioural couple therapy have centred on teaching members of couples to find ways to understand and accept one another in place of the blaming and attempted controlling prevalent in distressed couples. 'Acceptance is the missing link in traditional behavioral therapy,' say Jacobson and Christiansen (1996). 'The goal of empathic joining is to give both partners a different emotional view of their problems; ideally they will experience the problems through their partners' eyes' (Atkins et al. 2003: 294). In brief case examples, the authors illustrate facilitating the expression and hearing of 'soft' emotions such as hurt or fear rather than 'hard' emotions such as anger and frustration. Research on lasting change in couples supports couples' acceptance of one another over improved communication or exchange of caring behaviours (Jacobson 1995). Among their techniques are therapist expression of empathy in the form of 'I' statements. (Atkins et al. 2003). Jacobson and Christiansen use a 'non didactic format which emphasizes validation, compassion and a virtual absence of confrontation'. Starting from an entirely different direction, the work of Jacobson and Christiansen shows parallels to Carl Rogers' core conditions.

The therapist works through the barriers that keep them from unconditional positive regard in the following ways:

- Discuss all clients with whom you feel frustration with another colleague. Such dialogues help sort out your own judgements from your reception of your client. For example, I asked a female colleague for advice about the woman in a couple I was seeing. She had let herself go in many ways, had gained weight and – most importantly and seemingly in her power to change – she dressed and groomed herself terribly. Her husband was critical and withholding of affection or attention to her. What, I asked, would it be like if I met her briefly individually and asked her about her care of her appearance? (I have *only* had 35 years' experience!) My colleague, non-judgemental as always to me, asked how I thought a person might feel getting such feedback from another male along with the criticism and rejection she was feeling from her husband. 'Thank you,' I said, saying good-bye to that old familiar idea that people need lots of negative feedback.
- Work on your own expectations of yourself: if you judge yourself for not being able to change clients, they will feel it as a judgement on them.

●   Slow yourself down. Focusing on making contact with each client as they are in the moment (Condition 1) keeps judgement out of the centre of the room. Seeking to understand each person's inner frame of reference makes judgement irrelevant.

Case Example 4.2: Therapist's Empathic Acceptance Overcomes His Urgency to Confront and Instruct!

The therapist was increasingly frustrated by Sylvia's lack of awareness of the incongruence of her consistently disapproving or rejecting behaviour with her insistence that she loved and valued her husband. Sylvia seemed to hold to an unvarying belief that to give her husband credit for his grievances and unmet requests from her would put her back to the worthlessness and second-class citizenship of her early days staying home with her children when they were very young.

The therapist felt some urgency to confront her with her rigidity and lack of awareness of her own part in the couple's trouble. Fortunately, he was also aware that she could not receive any negative feedback without feeling attacked and shamed. In a previous session she had come in saying 'OK, let's find out what I've been doing wrong all these years', with a sense of someone walking to her own execution. Like most people suffering from insecurity – that is, most people – Sylvia could listen to feedback only within the safety of a caring relationship. Feedback to clients can be part of therapy only when or if they are able to see that feedback as a small part of a well-established caring relationship.

The therapist focused instead on how she was feeling in the present, after an argument that morning about their youngest son and a hockey accident (minor to her husband and an emergency to her). She felt trapped: either she should ignore her concerns about her kids and be silent (not a possibility), or she could risk her husband's disapproval for 'over-reacting'. The therapist spoke of each person's dilemma, Fred representing the side of wanting to keep their kids confident and unworried; Sylvia experiencing the dangers of life so keenly and feeling compelled to intervene in order to make their lives safe.

THERAPIST: You both represent something important for children, don't you? Each moment of possible danger for the kids makes you first afraid of Fred's disapproval and then angry at his lack of agreement with you. Is this the kind of situation in which you feel you can't win?

Billing Address
Neil Ward
Neil Ward Counselling
69 Buchanan Street
Glasgow, Lanarkshire G1 3HL
United Kingdom

Shipping Address
Neil Ward
Neil Ward Counselling
69 Buchanan Street
Glasgow, Lanarkshire G1 3HL
United Kingdom

Packing slip for
Your order of 4 January, 2012   Order ID 026-2926587-6037138   Packing slip number DKI1JXNrZN

Qty	Item	Bin
1	**The Practice of Person-Centred Couple and Family Therapy**	(** P-1-G74E341 **)
	Paperback. 023023318X	

This shipment completes your order.

13/DKI1JXNrZN/-1 of 1-//IH/same-uk/5758350/0105-15:00/0104 14:06/garysco Pack Type : A2

SYLVIA: Exactly. I'm upset about the kids. Then I'm upset about Fred's reaction. Every time something happens with the kids I look to him to back me up, but he always gets mad at me.

THERAPIST: Can you connect with this, Fred?

FRED: Absolutely.

THERAPIST: I think we are talking about something that happens again and again. The feeling that you cannot just relax with each other because there is always some incident about the kids that you can't get off your minds.

Later this session, Sylvia brought in the idea that they needed more times out together, just having fun without the kids. Sylvia thought this would be the key to making the therapy work. Her active contribution to the therapy may not have taken place in an atmosphere in which she perceived herself to be corrected. In subsequent sessions, she was more active and took many more initiatives. She identified Fred's behaviour that consistently prompted her withdrawal and anger; she followed this by more willing, welcoming words towards him. She showed a genuine interest in responding to his feedback.

In couple counseling, one path to facilitating a therapist's acceptance and understanding of their clients as well as clients' openness to one another is the oral history interview, best described by John Gottman (1999). Sometimes a couple, having made some progress in listening and expressing themselves, may not yet feel ready to tackle their most disturbing issues. Suggesting that they tell the story of their relationship is often welcomed as a preparation for exploring how to move on together. Box 4.2 describes this practice.

Box 4.2: Oral History Interviews

Researcher John Gottman (1999) offers the oral history interview as a tool for allowing couple conversation that can highlight resources for couple change. I have offered this possibility to many couples. Even when they choose to concentrate on their presenting problems, couples may feel encouraged when they add stories of past dilemmas to the conversation.

In the oral history interview, the clients tell the therapist and each other their experience of the relationship, event by event, year by year, from the beginning to the present. They collaborate on answering all the questions they or the therapist can think of. Among the details are how they met; how their feelings for each other progressed; when they became committed to one another and how that was expressed; when they married and moved in together; when and if they had children and what change occurred at that event or decision; how they dealt with their families of origin, money, careers and a hundred other things. Gottman offers a guide to what might be talked about that each therapist and couple may adapt (1999: 398). Stopping to explore emotional reactions or surprising perspectives allows couples to find the roots of their connection, trouble and resources in their cumulative story. This simple structure allows a client-centred dialogue between their past experience and their present dilemmas.

When clients tell the story of their relationship there are four possibilities that emerge:

- The clients engage together on a project that allows them to have a conversation that bypasses the state of distress between them, while remaining relevant to their way of functioning as a couple.
- The telling of their story to an interested, curious listener allows long-forgotten strengths, resolutions and attractions to emerge and influence their present thoughts, feelings and behaviours.
- A story about a relationship almost inevitably highlights experiences of overcoming conflicts and troubles that may be relevant to current difficulties.
- Their present distress is naturally put into the context of their overall life journey.

5. The therapist experiences an empathic understanding of the client's internal frame of reference and endeavours to communicate this experience to the client

At the centre of all good therapy, the client feels understood, heard about specifics and validated in their point of view. At the centre of relationship therapy, one person is not understood at the expense of their loved ones. At the centre of very helpful relationship therapy, the therapist shows an understanding of the whole situation in such a way that clients may feel more free to face the troubles of life together rather than as adversaries. They have 'a way to get on' (Rober 2005).

Once in a very unsuccessful first session, I confronted clients before really connecting with them. A consulting colleague reminded me of guiding principles that somehow I had found it easy to forget: 'Why didn't you just listen and reflect back what you heard them saying and let them decide what they would do with their predicament?'

Empathy in systems therapy means not only showing one client they are understood, but also translating your understanding of that client to their loved ones so that they have more permission to listen without being threatened. Person-centred family therapist Ned Gaylin describes 'interspace reflection' (2008), which includes articulating the way the whole communication – back and forth – appears to the therapist. Empathy makes acceptance real and accessible to our clients. What good is it if you think I am all right but don't really know me? 'Thank you for knowing me. Thank you for not confusing me with someone else,' wrote philosopher Martin Buber in response to greetings offered at his 80th birthday celebration (Coulson 1973).

Empathic listening is at the heart of 'slowing the process down', as we discussed in Chapter 3. Unlike a member of a distressed family, the therapist either understands each client who speaks or acknowledges that they don't understand. Either effort brings change into a system: each person deserves a hearing and listeners have to make an effort to learn by listening rather than assuming that they already know. Goolishian and Anderson have said, 'The therapist is always on the way to co-understanding with the client but never understands' (1992: 13). Those therapists, expressing a post-modern understanding of therapy that is similar to a person-centred approach as well as distinct from it, let go of 'prior knowledge' in favour of new dialogue that has never happened before. They parallel Rogers' discussion of the delight and 'surprise' clients sometimes have when they find themselves saying something they have never said before (Kirschenbaum and Henderson 1989).

In relationship therapy, the therapist not only offers empathy for clients but also facilitates their offering it to one another. One way I offer this is at the end of each session by requesting that each person share one thing they appreciate that another did during the session. Often, clients will say something that shows that the other has listened: 'He seemed to understand that I am on the same side as he is.' 'She let me talk about my mother without interrupting with criticism of her.' 'I was finally able to tell him what really bothered me about our business deal with my sister.'

Listening well in relationship therapy is a natural process as well as a learned art. Therapy thrives when the therapists are confident in their mission and humble in its execution. As an inexperienced therapist I was too tentative in carving space for reflective listening. The family conversation would roll over me like a wave and understanding would be drowned by clients doing what they do at home: talking over each other; preparing rebuttals before listening; imposing inaccurate theories about the other's meaning. *A therapist unwilling to interrupt should stay with individual therapy.* Therapist interruptions serve the purpose of giving listening a chance.

Experienced therapists, of course, can interrupt too much. They also know too much in advance and say it before the client does. What is intended as reassuring can quickly become annoying. Less experienced therapists can allow listeners' attention to wane in the presence of monologues. In Chapter 6 I will discuss the speaker/listener practice borrowed from earlier person-centred literature (Barrett-Lennard 1998: 93–6). In this taking-turns practice, the speaker is asked to stop speaking after a short enough time that the listener can remember sufficient of what was said to reflect it back.

In relationship therapy it is important to offer understanding not only of each individual but also of the whole system.

Case Example 4.3: Finding a Story That Two Cousins Can Share

Sometimes family therapy requires what Bozarth (1984) calls 'idiosyncratic empathy'. Two cousins, Glenn, 19 and Andy, 16, are in therapy with Pat, their mother and aunt, after the younger boy's mother had died. She had been living a life characterized by addiction and many illegal activities. It seemed likely that her son, Andy, had stolen from his cousin but could not admit it for reasons of pride and position. Glenn could not tolerate the other's not admitting the situation. The therapist said: 'Let me tell a story. Someone lives in another house with another parent. In that house, stealing outside and inside is part of life – not talked about, but the way things go. That person moves to another house where the customs are different. He may do things as he used to do even though he tries not to. He can't admit to doing things because that would make him a bad person. He's not a bad person even though he does things that make everyone angry. Is this a story that makes sense?'

The third-person narrative, influenced by White's idea of externalizing the problem, discussed in Chapter 1, allowed truth to be told with enough distance for dignity. Both boys and their mother/aunt agreed. The conversation was able to continue with both boys participating and able to continue to live together, not closely but with less tension and threat of a fight.

In an aid to empathy for a family, I take notes on a yellow pad without looking away from the clients. The handwriting is bad, but exact client words emerge that can serve as bridges. Recently in a family session a young man commented that he hated his mother's, saying he was 'only 16'. 'But you are *only 16!*' she said. 'Is the problem here that you think more that you are *almost 17?*' I asked her son. Later, he used the phrase 'almost an adult'. Earlier his mother had told him he was 'still a child'. Both were of course right and both were emphasizing the view of reality that informed their side of their dialogue. 'Almost an adult and still a child. Is this the difference we are all trying to figure out?' I asked, reading from my yellow pad.

6. *The communication to the client of the therapist's empathic understanding and unconditional positive regard is to a minimal degree achieved*

This condition is a sobering one for therapists: what do our clients think? Research indicates that therapists can often be wrong in their assumptions that their clients perceive them as empathic (Rogers 1980; Burns 2010). Most recommended but rarely practised is offering routine written client evaluations after each session. Sprenkle et al. (2009) have noted that regular evaluation is the only way the client experience of alliance with the therapist can be tracked. They further indicate that research on the strength of the client's relationship with the therapist is not only that the therapist is perceived as warm and accepting; as important is that the therapist seems in line with the *clients' goals* for the therapy. For example, if the clients came in to talk about sex and the therapist focuses on communication without relating it to improvements in sex, the clients are less satisfied, however much they might like the therapist. David Cain has written that being non-directive with clients who explicitly ask for direction can mean failing to be client centred (2010).

The following are reflections on connecting with the clients' experience of the therapy:

- Consider finding or designing evaluation forms (Burns 2010; also see David Burns' website, www.feelinggood.com; Miller and Duncan on http://talkingcure.com) that measure the conditions discussed above as well as the clients' experience of receiving help about their presenting predicament. The simple questions "What has been most helpful?" "What has been least helpful?" offer clients another way to have a voice in their own therapy. I do not do this often enough. Whenever I do offer it, I am provided with information, especially from the quietest members, about what they are thinking and feeling during the session. No clients have ever refused to accept an evaluation form. Those who are unenthused by such a project simply give the therapist a row of high marks and pass it back without comment.

- Relationship therapy may be compared to individual therapy the way acting in live theatre may be compared to film acting. A theatrical actor has to project voice and physical expression actively so that the audience is engaged and connected; subtlety can lead to misunderstanding. A film actor, aided by the camera and close-ups, needs to be restrained because every motion and voice inflection will have a strong effect on the more single-minded audience. The relationship therapist must engage, speak, ask for feedback, make summaries of what is occurring and otherwise assert a presence. All of the qualities of the therapist's presence will be ignored or subject to clients' projection if they are not clearly expressed. For example, when someone expresses anger, accusation, sadness or any other strong feeling, the therapist's silence can be interpreted as agreement, indifference or lack of attention depending on the circumstances.

- Taking time at the end of sessions to check in with clients on what they feel was important in that session allows clients to enter a reflective mode. Often they can take charge of the learning in the session by informing the therapist about what was important to them; they can redirect the therapy by expressing whether or not the process was congruent with their reason for being there.

- This therapist sometimes does a telephone follow-up after his own reflection on a session. A call to ask 'How did the session land on you?' may allow clients who received negative feedback from other clients to integrate their experience with a brief contact with a supportive therapist. Sometimes the therapist may share a perception about a client's feelings at the end of the session. This experience of the therapist caring without rescuing can deepen the client's courage for the difficult passage they may be experiencing. For example, a mother may feel ganged up on by her son and his father – a good experience of bonding for them but a sacrifice for her.

Clients feel comfortable to do their work when they experience the conditions described above. Even the therapist's personal faults cannot stand in the way of clients who feel safe to be themselves without having to lose or harm their loved ones. One client who was seen both individually and as part of a couple once brought her elderly mother for a family therapy session, as much to meet me as anything else. She told her mother: 'The one thing that Charles will never do is tell me what to do.' In fact, I have shared strong ideas and opinions with this client on far more than one occasion. Fortunately, she received my attitude of respect and my willingness to listen rather than any limit to trust in her own judgement and right to decide.

The six conditions of the person-centred approach are a natural corollary of Rogers' 'actualizing tendency' (see Chapter 1): they facilitate the clients' own movement in the direction of becoming themselves.

Conclusion

Rogers' core conditions offer six pathways to assessing the quality of a therapist's presence. Individual therapists who are familiar with these conditions can reflect on how they translate into the medium of relationship therapy. Couple and family therapists can renew their attention to the quality of their client relationships whenever their work becomes too therapist or technique centred. Recent emphasis on session-by-session client written evaluation can give the clients a more active role in helping the therapist tune in to their experiences.

Chapter 5 will feature a dialogue between a person-centred approach and the unique tasks of couple therapy.

5

Couple Therapy:
A Person-Centred Way

This chapter, focused on therapy with couples in general, is the first of three chapters describing work with different types of client. Chapter 6 will discuss therapy with sexual minorities, focusing particularly on gay and lesbian couples, while Chapter 7 presents therapy with children and teenagers.

'We fight because you're like you are and I am like I am' is how one client described conflict with his spouse. Couples in distress often do not listen well to one another, do not accept the other without conditions and frequently do not see the other as authentic or themselves as safe to be their congruent selves. Members of couples come to therapy looking for a secure place to stand as they attempt to find a connection in the midst of confusion, frustration and, often, unspoken loss.

Here, we discuss the initial description of therapy to couples and the unique purpose of couple therapy: attention to each person *and* to the relationship. Presentation of common reasons for therapy and a brief summary of John Gottman's research on couples will lead to reflection on a person-centred approach to relationships. I discuss the way in which core ideas from couple and family therapy literature as well as the 'speaker/listener' process affect my day-to-day work with couples. A case description shows a person-centred way of meeting with a couple over time. I reflect on similarities and differences with the emotion focused couple therapy of Susan Johnson (2004; Moser and Johnson 2008) and Leslie Greenberg (Greenberg and Johnson 1986; Greenberg and Golden 2008). The chapter closes with descriptions of the kind of client initiatives that are a positive outcome of a therapeutic experience.

Common Expectations in Couple Therapy

When clients call and ask what couple therapy is like, I tell them it is an opportunity for each person to say what he or she truly wants or is troubled by without driving the other person out of the room or into a state of defensiveness. With these words I affirm each person's right to be heard and understood; I also ask them to commit implicitly to a way of communication that is respectful and opens the door to dialogue rather than to a one-way practice of complaining. I usually tell people that it is not a place just to have a fight while paying a therapist. They can do that at home, for free. (Usually callers laugh, often having feared this.)

In this dialogue with potential clients I am often asked whether I will give them tools for better communication; whether I have hope that relationships can improve; and whether I see people alone or together. I answer yes to the first question, with the understanding that my main purpose is to respond to what people are looking for. I do believe strongly that relationships can improve, although that depends on the commitment of the clients to make that happen. Regarding the format of the therapy, I say that I usually see a couple together as the primary process, but I am open to their wishes to be seen alone from time to time, including at the beginning. How we begin, individual or couple, is up to the clients although, if there are several individual therapy sessions, I may recommend another therapist for the couple sessions.

Person-centred couple therapy is a process that draws on each client's ability to find their own way to understand, express themselves, contribute, connect and, sometimes, forgive. Couple therapy also requires therapist structuring, translation and commentary. If the therapy is helpful, the therapist is seen as supportive and understanding of each client, although that is not their only focus. The relationship therapist must carry one more expectation than the individual therapist: *the hope that they would be helpful for the relationship.* Couples look for a way to care for their relationship without losing themselves. They may expect us to:

- frame conversations so that they are possible between people frustrated by their inability to be understood;
- help a couple restore what has been lost between them in a crisis or series of troubles;
- offer a way of proceeding when the relationship 'gets ugly', as more than one person has described their experience of causing one another suffering;
- facilitate the reappearance of love and support in their relationships;

- facilitate the problem-solving ability of people in the relationship, or, at least, help them to treat one another with respect in the face of irresolvable problems (Gottman and Silver 1999);
- release one or both individuals from an atmosphere that stifles growth and self-actualization without their having to lose the other.

With some couples, there is one person less committed to the relationship, who may not expect it to work, who may even know that it can't work because of their own behaviour, for instance continuing in an affair or refusing to spend time with their partner. They also, nonetheless, hope for something from the therapist: that they may be able to rediscover the ability to commit to the relationship or that they would make the couple break-up more positive; that they can have a way of proceeding as separate people with common responsibilities, most importantly children, as well as common friends and loved ones, shared work or assets. Influenced by Carl Rogers, I never assume not only that I know what is best for a couple, but also that I know in which direction they will turn. Clients surprise me: it is their lives in which we are engaging.

Common Client Reasons for Couple Therapy

Here are ten reasons couples come for therapy. They are the impetus, motivation and driving force for change, as well a focus of energy in a field of many unspoken disappointments, confusions, losses, fears and limitations. Clients rarely come for existential exploration. Qualities such as hopes, joys, plans and the ability to be intimate seem like distant memories, but the therapist can be aware of their possibilities in the shadow of the troubles. Couples may need to say what is wrong to someone who takes them seriously before they can open the door to changing their situation. It is very important that the therapist listen carefully to both trouble and implied goals and respond accordingly. To fail to do so may leave the clients feeling unheard and weaken the therapeutic alliance (Sprenkle et. al. 2009). On the other hand, the therapist attempts to orient to the whole relationship, including their reasons for being together, in order to put the current trouble into context. Common reasons for therapy include the following:

- Something has happened – an affair, an attempt at an affair or a conversation about no longer loving – that is devastating for one member of the couple and guilt producing for the other.

- One fight too many or too fierce for a couple that makes the relationship seem in an emergency and unable to continue as it is.
- A difficulty with a child or children (especially in a blended family) that has led one or both to feel that children will be harmed if something is not done.
- One person in the relationship who feels that the other has been mistreating them or neglecting them for far too long and will no longer stay in the relationship unless the other person changes.
- Some chronic trouble, unemployment, sickness or radical financial differences that can no longer be avoided.
- Alcohol or drug abuse, which appears in any and all forms.
- Sexual disappointment for one or both partners.
- An arrangement based on one view of gender authority, equality, role definition and involvement that is no longer possible for one or both people.
- One person who feels unloved and expresses their unhappiness in criticism of the other, who then withdraws and is even less expressive of love. This is no longer bearable for one of them.
- Fear of missing out on happiness that becomes urgent: each person feels truly unable to accept the other as they seem to be without risking their future happiness, if not their dignity.

From 1975 to the present, John Gottman and his associates have done more research on heterosexual couples than anyone in history (Gottman 1999). His research has had the following elements:

- The videotaping of couples at an apartment at the University of Washington for every minute of a whole weekend, except when in the bathroom or bedroom. The couples were also measured for physiological reactions to different conversations and experiences.
- Questionnaires and interviews of thousands of couples, including those in the above experiences.
- Longitudinal follow-up on couples for over 25 years.
- Correlation of couples' behaviour on tape, their subjective impressions of self and relationship, their reported happiness and distress and the outcome of their relationship. Still together? Together and happy? Together and distressed?

From this steady collection of data, Gottman and associates have much to say about what happens in successful and unsuccessful relationships. For example, they have found these characteristics:

- A steady cascade of criticism, defensiveness, contempt and stonewalling (refusing to speak or respond to a topic that is urgent to another) predicts termination of a relationship.
- Distressed couples have a pattern of 'harsh start-up': bringing up topics in an angry, blaming way by one partner and failure to 'accept influence' by the other.
- Non-distressed couples have the same amount of troubles as distressed couples, but have a five to one proportion of positive experiences to negative.
- In general, males are more physiologically distressed by conflict and take a long time to recover from it, while females (if there is no physical danger) tend not to be distressed by conflict but are greatly distressed if they feel ignored or shut out.
- People in long and happy relationships have as many irresolvable issues than others, but somehow manage to face them with respect, flexibility and humour.

Presenting some of these findings for the first time at the American Association of Marriage and Family Therapists' annual conference in 1989, Gottman received sustained applause from the more than three-quarters female audience when he announced the unexpected finding that *men who did housework tended to be happier than those who did not!*

Since 2000, Gottman and his wife Julie have been focusing on the effects on a relationship of the birth or adoption of children (Gottman and Gottman 2007). Finding that two-thirds of couples show significant distress after the arrival of a child, the Gottmans have developed educational programmes to facilitate this transition. (It is my experience that couples may suffer from unresolved issues from this transition years and even decades later.) The Gottmans have also completed a 13-year study of gay and lesbian relationships that will be discussed in Chapter 7.

Towards a Person-Centred Couple Therapy

In Chapter 1 I described key ideas that are my constant companions as a relationship therapist. I will now describe five of those ideas as they apply to work with couples.

- *The dynamic of the core conditions of the person-centred approach.* The attitude of acceptance of the couple and their predicament is central to work with couples. There is often a lot of shame: that their relationship requires therapy; that they couldn't do it on their own. There is often fear that the therapy would make things worse and that the therapist would take sides. Frequently couples bring a fight or, as colleague Jamey Collins says, 'A power struggle walks in the room with them' (personal communication). Empathy – expressed by the desire to find out what each feels and cares about, independent of who is right or should be in charge – can allow safety and disarm clients so that they can join the therapist in listening to the other as a person, not an opponent. Finally, the therapist must seem *congruent* so that the couple can trust their most important relationship with them as an ally and witness who is not pursuing an agenda different from their own. Perceived realness, as Rogers has said, allows other therapist qualities to make sense.

- *Reframing*. A couple are stuck in a vision of their relationship that creates false dichotomies: win or lose; be independent or be loved; be right or be wrong; reach agreement or separate; stay the same or lose the relationship; my kids or you. The therapist facilitates a process in which space can be created for conversation that allows more diversity, differentiation or adaptation to change. Reframing is really the shared process of liberating a couple from an impossible perspective. Externalizing the problem is an important way of reframing. Talking about 'the fight' or 'the great depression' can allow couples ways to separate themselves from habits that make them strangers to one another. One couple gave me the concept of 'the old normal' to describe the way of life that led to near divorce and 'the new normal' to describe their new way of seeing and acting towards one another. Jacobson and Christiansen in their adapted behavioral therapy talk about 'the formulation', which is a reframing of the couple's distress that both can relate to and work to change (1996).

- *Dominant story/alternate story*. Each couple in distress is trapped in a dominant story of frustration, feeling unloved or unfairly attacked, and a sense of inability to make things better without sacrificing core values and needs. There is a sense of hopelessness that is in the foreground and a sense of efficacy or success seems a distant memory. Couple therapy calls attention to alternate stories, even small practices or events in which things are going well. Almost always, I give clients a small notebook in which they may record any event in which things were expected to go badly but instead went well.

- *Holding and expressing awareness of human development and consequent change in roles, boundaries and hierarchy*. Each individual changes as a couple live through the events of life together. Change can first appear as a threat to the relationship and especially be expressed in a sense of increased or decreased closeness, dependency, adventurousness, stability, submissiveness, availability, shared interests and available time (the feeling of too little time, or too much) and power to make decisions. Many couple conflicts may be legitimately reframed as transitions that need to be renegotiated. Case 5.1 includes shared reflection on the couple's lifespan experience as an important part of finding a reconstituted relationship.

● *Enactments* (Butler and Gardner 2003; Butler et al. 2008; Johnson 2008). After a couple become secure in the therapeutic relationship, a contrast often emerges between their ability to talk in the session and their fighting and frustration at home. Inviting the couple to bring their conflicts into the session allows for a safe way to experiment with new understanding and a new way of getting through their predicaments. This is the opposite of having a fight, in that the therapist and the clients are observers and participants. Usually the couple briefly demonstrate how they talk about the issue at home. Any one of the three people can stop the action to explore feelings and thoughts. The couple are then invited to explore what they would prefer to happen and then have the same conflict again, incorporating listening, a softer expression of needs and concerns and an understanding of validity in the other person's point of view.

This therapist is person centred while using the tools and perspectives of couple therapy. Listening and client direction have priority; and use of imagination in co-creating new perspectives is responsive to the goals that clients bring to therapy.

In the Mind of a Couple Therapist

I study every therapist or researcher I can, in books, workshops, seminars and on compact discs. Their work is with me as background, as questions for dialogue, as possibilities even while I focus on what each client has to say.

Here are some ideas that I have mind when I meet couples:

● I believe that couple therapy helps if members of couples are allowed both to express their own experience as well as to seek a wider, clearer perspective on the forces that shape their relationship.

- Each person wants something understood and is frustrated when it is not understood by their partner and touched when it is understood. Each person has something they 'want to get across to the other' (Wile 1993).

- Acceptance of the other person as they are and acceptance of their own choices, including the choice of that other person, allows for understanding and change. 'What's different?' I once asked a usually grim and combative couple. 'Oh, I stopped being angry at him,' the woman in the couple told me. 'She really has,' said her husband, whose steady willingness to care about her had had an effect on that anger.

- Each person has to deal with that emotional complex called 'feeling sorry for yourself; as part of life (O'Leary 2006). If they expect that disappointment and sadness are part of life, they can face them without having to project then onto their partner. If, in session, one partner can face sadness about their life without blaming their partner or their partner feeling blamed, a couple may move on with greater harmony.

- Couples who have a baby together must face losses, fundamental changes and misunderstandings in their relationship that otherwise could haunt them for years if not decades after a child arrives. (See Gottman and Gottman 2007 for research and information about this all-important time in family development.)

- Couples who are already parents before entering a relationship need to be clear about expectations regarding sharing as well as *not* sharing responsibility for their children's well-being. The roots of many struggles in blended families lie in undefined roles and boundaries before the families move in with each other. Many power struggles in stepfamilies are the results not of ill-will or incompetence, but of people trying to live with inherently impossible expectations (Visher and Visher 1982, 1987; Doherty 1999).

- Couples often have apparently impossible conversations remaining unspoken between them. The process of therapy can allow them to expose those conversations to fresh air without forcing a premature or unattainable resolution of them. All conversations are made more possible if the couple have frequent, *easy* conversations, asking about each other's interests, efforts and thoughts.

- All marriages are cross-cultural even if the couple grew up next door to one another and share the same ethnic and religious background and even the same gender (Falicov 1986). Even then, their genetics and temperaments may still create a cultural divide. Therefore a male must cross over to the land of the female; a verbally fluent person must cross to the land of the person of action; an introvert must cross over to the land of an extravert; a timid/avoidant person must cross over to the land of the bold/curious; an emotionally expressive person must cross over to the land of the emotionally withholding – and, of course, vice versa.

● A long marriage means many acts of resetting expectations, many virtues and many decisions. One decision is whether or not to forgive the person you have lived with (Treadway 2008). Despite many acts of kindness and many moments of happiness, there are, inevitably, many disappointments, missed opportunities and hurts, intentional or unintentional. There are, of course, definite cost/benefit analyses that take place in every relationship (Stuart 1980). There is something else as well: a decision to love, to commit unconditionally; to work on problems from inside a partnership rather than as an external judge of a partner.

A simple tool can become powerful in a safe setting. The practice of taking turns in actively listening to one another, described in Box 5.1, can make some of these tasks and practices come alive.

Box 5.1: Speaker/Listener

The practice of speaker/listener or active listening is an originally person-centred idea (Guerney 1977; Barrett-Lennard 1998) that is also found in behavioural couple therapy (Gottman 1994) and Imago couple therapy (Jamey Collins, personal communication). The way I use it, each member of a couple is given five or more turns to say 'what they would really like the other person to understand'. The other person is carefully coached to 'have only the job of listening and understanding what your partner is saying. You don't have to agree or disagree, only repeat back what you hear them saying.' Sometimes the therapist offers suggestions about what to address to start the process, but the heart of it is clients speaking and being heard by their loved ones. Many clients take this opportunity and meet one another in a way that bypasses their habits of argument or monologue.

I frequently suggest this when clients seem stuck or an irresistible argument or irre-solvable problem dominates the dialogue. Some clients become tearful, as though seeing an old friend who has been missing for several years. As my colleague Jamey Collins says, 'It can feel very good.' Others need coaching and support to manage to listen rather than editorialize or rebut. Some are simply not able to leave their own position long enough to listen without intruding with their own reaction. Finally, some couples feel too vulnerable for such an intimate meeting and put it off to another time.

This practice captures the heart of person-centred couple therapy: the therapist is really active while, paradoxically, each person's unique sharing is at the centre. As with many suggestions, clients benefit either from engaging in the practice or making a choice not to. Often I offer clients the choice of continuing the process as they are now in it, using speaker/listener or engaging in an enactment (described in Chapter 1 and below, in which they bring a fight or trouble from home and duplicate it, with my active assistance, in the office).

John Gottman (1999) has commented that used at home, speaker/listener can become counter-productive and recommends against it. He finds that actively listening to a partner complaining about you can produce dysphoria and distance. I have had some similar experiences. I offer the technique for use primarily in my office and suggest appreciations as part of the content as partners listen to one another. If it works for them, clients may try it on their own as they choose.

Another Approach to Therapy Influenced by Carl Rogers

Both Susan Johnson and Leslie Greenberg credit client-centred therapy and Carl Rogers, along with other humanist approaches, in the development of the therapy described in Box 5.2. I will describe parallels and differences between a person-centred approach and this related model of couple therapy.

Box 5.2: Emotion Focused Couple Therapy

Originated by Leslie Greenberg and Susan Johnson (1986) and developed currently by each on somewhat different paths (Greenberg and Goldman 2008a, b; Moser and Johnson 2008), emotion focused couple therapy (EFCT) is currently the most research-validated approach to work with relationships in the field today (Johnson and LeBow 2000). Its roots are squarely in client-centered therapy (Johnson 2008). In fact, it is a way of allowing the effects of the person-centred approach, especially empathy and acceptance, to influence the way people are treated in relationships. EFCT provides descriptions of the most common patterns of relationship difficulty, as well as a structure within which blaming language can be translated into a deeper expression of primary feelings such as hurt, fear and loneliness.

According to Susan Johnson (2008), EFCT combines client-centred therapy, systems thinking and attachment theory. The approach focuses on the loss of emotional connection between partners. Briefly described, it is a three-stage, nine-step process that focuses on:

1. *Cycle disengagement*: that is, awareness and diffusion of conflict and distancing by person-to-person empathy and collaborative definition of frustrating pattern (see slowing the process down and thinking meta, as described in Chapter 1).
2. *Withdrawer re-engagement*: having related couple conflict to emotional cut-off due to attachment issues, couples are gradually coached in enactments (see Chapter 1) to learn to express vulnerability and caring to one another.
3. *Blamer softening*: as couples express and meet one another's needs for connection, security is increased and clients are able to seek loving attention and cooperation without falling into accusation and harshness.

I find emotion focused couple therapy confirming and helpful. I think that my work is most like this approach in its emphasis on the kind of listening that draws out the primary feelings, such as hurt, fear, sadness, disappointment, hopelessness and grief, that underlie reactive feelings and behaviours such as anger, accusation, frustration, attempts to control, argumentative assertions, suspicion and jealousy. Here are four parallels:

*   In a person-centred way, the therapist goes out towards each person in supportive endorsement of their need for understanding, caring and love.
*   Johnson's description (2008) of a very common heterosexual pattern is important: a female, not feeling loved, becomes critical and negative; her male partner withdraws in the face of her anger; she feels even angrier in response to that withdrawal.
*   The need for the least engaged partner to be brought into the therapy and have their sense of being criticized and blamed acknowledged is emphasized (see Chapter 4 regarding 'psychological contact').
*   Johnson's work is close to Rogers' intent in two ways: each person feels not only heard but validated as themselves; secondly, she offers them the possibility of offering one another the anxiety-reducing, growth-producing conditions that Rogers asks of therapists.

Leslie Greenberg (Greenberg and Goldman 2008a, b) offers additional useful perspectives that I often share with couples as a way of describing common relationship development. He includes the emphasis on attachment and connection highlighted in Johnson's work. He also offers two other motivations that are important in understanding each couple's journey: identity maintenance and control; and attraction and liking. These are the two other systems that are important in a couple's growth, distress or recovery.

This approach parallels the person-centred approach in the following ways:

*   It privileges emotional experience over behavioural technique.
*   It facilitates personal exploration of the experience of connection and disconnection.

- It bypasses facts of interpersonal events in favour of understanding the emotional meanings of those events.
- It emphasizes client-to-client, in-the-room events rather than therapist-centred 'talking about'.
- It has empathic reflection' as its basic technique (Johnson 2008).

EFCT adds the following to the person-centred approach:

- It offers a theory of love.
- It provides a basic structure to add predictability to the process and thus reduce therapist and client anxiety, as well as offering a map.
- It suggests more books and workshops and supervising therapists for developing couple therapists than are found, at this time, in the person-centred world. In the absence of an explicitly person-centred workshop, I am likely to recommend attendance at workshops offered by Johnson or Greenberg or their associates.
- It provides information about recurring themes in couple experience that can become part of the language of empathy and commentary and couple empathic guesses about the narrative of the situation.
- It offers tools for 'de-escalation' that any couple and family therapist will need in order to proceed.
- It encourages enactments: in-session experiences in which clients relive common impasses or practise new possible conversations.

Nevertheless, a person-centred therapist may differ from this approach because:

- A person-centred therapist follows the clients rather than any pre-existing structure, however compelling.
- A person-centred therapist does not assume that any one pattern will apply to clients.
- If therapists are like me, they may find that whenever they follow a step-by-step agenda, even lightly, they can get out of touch with listening to clients and more into the process of fitting them into a framework.

Case Example 5.1 describes a person-centred perspective in the long-term couple therapy of two people who have been together for 35 years. It is the longest case presentation in this book and I chose it because it illustrates the quality of impossibility that sometimes enters the room along with some clients, as well as the importance of the therapist not making assumptions about whether or not a marriage can survive.

Case Example 5.1: A Couple Enter Therapy When All Hope for the Relationship Has Ended

Rick and Lucilla, a couple in their fifties who had been married over 30 years, came to see me after Lucilla discovered that Rick had been having an affair with a co-worker.

LUCILLA: I think the marriage is over. I am not going to live like this any more. I am getting ready to divorce him. I can't believe he came to this session, by the way.

THERAPIST: The affair has somehow confirmed what you have already thought. Your marriage is over. Yet you are here, likely to divorce him but not quite ready to. You are curious about why he is here in the session.

THERAPIST: *(Later)* And here you are, Rick, you have come here even though Lucilla is getting ready to divorce you.

RICK: I screwed up. I admit it. Maybe she should divorce me. I don't know. Maybe the marriage is over. I don't know. But I don't want it to be. She can kick me out if she wants to but I don't want to leave. Hey, we've been getting along better than we have in years!

The therapist listens. The couple talk about the marriage ending, yet instead of ending it, they are here in the therapist's office. Curiosity, openness to what each is looking for, desire to know each person as they are – all of these are important elements in the therapy. The therapist is also motivated by belief in process: something can come of this meeting. In keeping with the common factors of effective relationship therapy described in Chapter 3, the conversation slows the process down so that complexities may emerge.

Lucilla told her story with tears that alternated with a sense of wonder at a new-found strength and certainty that she had been paradoxically experiencing after learning of a series of lies and of Rick's relationship with another woman. For this couple, the detected affair was only one of several over the years that Lucilla had formerly accepted as one of the conditions of her marriage. Her husband had, this time, made barely believable promises to stay faithful. She alternated tears and expression of hurt with a look of amused puzzlement that he and she were actually in therapy together.

LUCILLA: I think I am going to divorce him, but we have been having more talks and doing more things together than we ever have, so we'll see.

RICK: *(loud of voice but very friendly in manner and easy with laughter)* Bet you can't figure us out. Here we are talking and getting along and we're probably going to get divorced! *(Lucilla laughs)*

The therapist lets go of urgency to advise or explain the couple, but accepts them as they are. *In the next session the following conversation takes place:*

LUCILLA: I don't know. I'm probably going to divorce him. There is no marriage here. It's funny; we have been talking more than we have for years. We are even having sex. I don't know. I know I can't trust him. But we'll see. I probably won't do anything until after Christmas. Then, after the new year, I will divorce him.

RICK: *(laughs at the humour of their ambiguous situation)* I guess she means it. I don't know. I screwed up. I can't ask for another chance. I don't know what she wants to do but I don't think I want a divorce.

The couple present many irresolvable issues and I seek to empathize with each, as both speaker and listener. I make sure that neither dominates the session.

Lucilla is very angry at Rick for his spending on cars, entertaining and recreational equipment, while she keeps them afloat financially by careful planning and little spending on herself. Rick entertains his friends at the home and in their large, secluded garden, while she, excluded and not approving of their heavy drinking and loud voices, is kept awake and silent and lonely in her own home. Rick has complaints about Lucilla. He is the family's principal cook and housekeeper. She leaves things around everywhere and is disorganized. Rick is also very involved with their grandson who, with their son and daughter-in-law, lives in their basement.

Lucilla spends part of each session crying about what she has endured. She also laughs in wonder at her clarity in taking charge of her life and at Rick, whom she enjoys and finds interesting.

LUCILLA: You still have that Mercedes that I'm still paying for; you promised you would sell the MG to pay for it. It's my money but I don't have any say in it at all.

THERAPIST: There is a list of things that bother you. It's like you are mad at him for the way he has been acting and you are mad at yourself for letting this happen.

RICK: Well, let me explain about those cars. I did have a buyer for the MG, but he wasn't able to get a loan for it so you [Lucilla] didn't want me to let him have it *(and so on in a long explanation)* but, hey, I admit it. I have been selfish. I have been used to getting my own way. She's more responsible than I am.

THERAPIST: So here you are. Your wife is angry with you. Those cars are important to you, but your wife thinks you have been taking things you want without caring about her.

RICK: Well, I do care about her. Listen, we have been living separately for a long time. She goes her way and I go mine and maybe I have gone my way more extravagantly than she has! *(They both laugh)*

The therapist is not in the business of labelling this couple or even changing the way they have lived. The question is whether the dialogue that both seem committed to will lead them towards more connection; to a sense that divorce is the best outcome; or to acceptance of a relationship that is more than friendship but less than marriage. Rick is extraverted and launches himself into long explanations. Lucilla, though she is the initiator of the therapy and the injured party, has less opportunity to speak unless the therapist stops Rick and invites her to speak.

LUCILLA: It is not my house.

RICK: Hey, it is your house, but it's my house too. I can have anyone around that I want and so can she. I have asked her a hundred times if I have asked her once, if she would join us. She always says no. 'Why should I? They are not my friends. I don't have any say in when they come and when they leave. I don't have any say in how much they drink.' I don't stop her from her socializing, but she shouldn't stop mine.

THERAPIST: Rick, I don't think Lucilla was finished.

LUCILLA: Well, it's going to change. I have already come out and told people to go home and I am going to keep doing it. It's not my house if I can't get to sleep because your friends are still talking loudly.

RICK: She is changing! She did that! I didn't like it, but she did it and I didn't say anything.

The couple face a crisis. After the third therapy session, Lucilla found out that Rick had, in fact, made an attempt to get back in touch with the other woman.

LUCILLA: *(with some tears)* Now I know I will divorce him. I was starting to wonder, maybe I can trust him. Don't you know how much what you did hurts me?

RICK: Yes, I know I hurt you. I fucked up. I don't even know why I called her or what I would have done. I'm mixed up. The funny thing is, I love her [Lucilla] more now, even though I do stuff like this. A few months ago, I wouldn't have cared what happened but now I do.

LUCILLA: I know I can't trust him. I don't know what I want to do with him, but I know I can't trust him.

The reader may have an opinion about whether Rick is sincere in his regret or if, even if he is, Lucilla would be wise to continue to trust him. The therapist remains curious about what this couple will want, what this event meant. The therapist did not assume that the couple would even want a next appointment. They readily asked for one.

In the next session the conversation continued.

LUCILLA: Well, we've been getting along better than ever. We have been out to dinner; he hasn't had friends over as much. We are actually talking. I'm still going to divorce him because I know I can't trust him, but I'm going to do it in my own time.

LUCILLA: (later) He's always been fun. I will always enjoy him. He just hasn't been a good husband. *(Rick laughs enthusiastically)*

The couple came in every two weeks for about six months, then stopped for a summer and resumed for another few months. Two Christmases came and went and Lucilla did not divorce Rick.

Among events in the therapy were these:

● Their adult children came in for a session. They were uniformly supportive of their mother and at once explicitly disapproving about what hurt Rick had caused her and admiring of Lucilla's newfound assertiveness, freedom and clarity. Rick handled their criticism with a moderate amount of defensiveness, but was affectionate and engaged with them. A picture of the marriage was supported by this meeting: Lucilla's long-established silence and forbearance and Rick's sense of being able to do whatever he wants and still have a secure marriage. A new pattern was supported: Lucilla finds her voice and takes charge of her life; Rick is confronted with a choice between his old way of life and the survival of his marriage. (The children assist them in 'thinking meta', as described in Chapter 3.)

- They told the story of their long marriage and the families they had both left at very young ages because of abuse and neglect. Neither of their fathers had stayed involved with the families; both of their mothers had leaned on them for responsibilities beyond their years. They had both managed education and long-term jobs without support. Lucilla had certainly over-functioned and Rick under-functioned in financial responsibility and care of the children. They both loved their children and grandchildren and shared both affection and desire to help, as well as desire for the children to take charge of their own lives and move out!

- Rick attended meetings in which he was held accountable for past misbehaviour and was told that his current behaviour needed to change. His showing up without demanding to 'put the past behind us' was an important indication of the marriage's chance of survival. (Clients who quickly demand forgiveness and trust after infidelity or lack of commitment show little promise of relationship repair (Abrahms-Spring 2005.)

- They gradually reported more activities together. They spent several evenings a week with each other, watched television together, started taking trips together (previously Rick travelled alone and Lucilla visited family or stayed at home).

- Lucilla had more say in the comings and goings of visitors. More of her friends were invited to the home.

- Importantly, Lucilla reclaimed Christmas for the couple. She replaced Rick's party for his friends who usually stayed over on Christmas Eve, Christmas Day and more with her own, more family-oriented gatherings. She and Rick were co-hosts of a gathering of which both were in charge.

I characterize the role of the therapist in this process in the following ways:

- He did not attempt either to save the marriage or to advise a divorce; he was the facilitator of a conversation leading to an outcome that would be their responsibility.

- He was needed in order to give each person a chance to speak; to empathize with their positions as they saw it; to give them the experience of a conversation in which both spoke and both were heard.
- He was aware from the beginning that Lucilla felt able to take charge of her life, on her own terms, and that his facilitating room for the couple to respond to this change was the key to the therapy.
- He offered tools for communication and problem solving at home as well as questions that allowed for reflection on their families of origin and the past course of their marriage.
- He facilitated conversation about many lost moments and injuries and each person's ability to forgive and accept the other in the present.
- He genuinely liked the couple and there was a sense that they could reflect on their past lives and current choices in a non-judgemental atmosphere.

Person-Centred Therapy and the 'Space in Between'

Person-centred therapists do not tell people what to do; they 'create a climate' in which clients can facilitate change. The more couples experience and are able to find their own practice of empathy and acceptance and feel more confident that they can be openly themselves, the more the couple's atmosphere can change. 'I feel a burden has been lifted,' said one client regarding freedom from pressure to be right or immediately solve a problem.

Scheiffer (2008) makes a distinction between each individual, who is a rich unfathomable world in themselves, and the 'space in between' – how they interact – that must be looked after and that is like a garden that either allows living things to grow or stifles and neglects them. Each person is a whole culture, a whole system of meaning, inevitably not the same as their partner or relatives. Sheiffer relates concepts of respect, awareness of differentness and curiosity as important virtues in intimate relationships. She says that we must 'cross a bridge' to visit the people we love rather than assume that we understand them because of our knowledge of our particular world. The concept of 'the between', which she derived from Martin Buber, is an alternative to the power struggle over control and correctness that can dominate relationships.

Rogers' core conditions nurture the 'space in between'. Couple therapists can ask clients to do for each other what the person-centred conditions ask therapists to do for them. Clients are asked to seek to understand the other person's internal frame of reference (Condition 5: empathy) rather than fail to accept the other because of judgements of their motivation. They do not have to agree with it in order to accept it as valid for the other. Condition 2, understanding how a loved one can be in a state of incongruence rather than holding it against them, can bring wisdom into the relationship. This second condition suspends the illusion that we can be completely sure of another person's reliability: my partner may or may not have perfect motivation for this new stage in our lives, but I can respond to it as if it is sincerely meant and see what happens. Clients have a right to make choices about whether or not to trust. Clients sometimes intently look at one another as though their whole future depends on the other's trustworthiness: 'Are you real? Can I trust you? Can I depend on your words?' They reflect the need for Condition 3 (congruence) to be present for their partner as well as for the therapist. Couple therapists Susan Johnson, John Gottman and Neal Jacobson all write from entirely different approaches about the importance of accepting, prizing and unconditional love (Condition 4: unconditional positive regard).

How Couples Change for the Better: A Vision of Good Outcomes in Therapy

- A couple stays up talking later than they have for a long, long time or perhaps ever, and talk more deeply than they have talked in a long, long time or perhaps ever, with more openness and mutual understanding than they have had for a long, long time or perhaps ever.
- One member of a couple returns to the level of loving behaviour that characterized their early relationship and the other appreciates it, becomes more trusting and eventually reciprocates. It would be nice, but is not always necessary for both members of a couple to change at first. One member of the couple, persisting in a change, allows for the other to be safe to change or to attain clarity about their willingness to continue the relationship under any conditions.
- Impossible words or behaviour seem at first less horrible, then less infuriating, then less hurtful, then less intentional and finally not so impossible after all.

- Blame is not the first reaction to an unfortunate event, nor the second, nor the third.
- Children get older, money becomes less scarce, one or both partners feel better, an annoying job ends, an irritating neighbour or family member moves or passes on and, one day, a bitter conflict seems less urgent, troubling or fearsome.
- Something soft, generous, genuine or disarming occurs, often in the midst of an external event, which allows greater compassion, humour, closeness and understanding. Barry Duncan (2005) tells the story of a couple who were estranged and getting ready for the end of their relationship. They had long since started sleeping in separate rooms. When a couple were visiting them and had stayed so late and drunk so much that there was no alternative but to invite them to stay overnight, the couple were forced to sleep together in the only remaining bedroom. Together without a choice, a new conversation began along with their physical closeness. They did not again return to sleeping in separate bedrooms.
- A man learns to listen more with less defensiveness, show up more and act more like a member of a team. His partner is less critical, no longer reaches the worst conclusions about his motivation, is less overwhelmed and lets go of more control.
- Both ask for something more gently, say yes more and say no with greater kindness (Treadway 2008) and there is the implication that future yeses are possible.
- Hopefulness replaces fear. Curiosity becomes as possible as anger. Genuine humour that includes laughing at oneself replaces sarcasm, caricature, cynicism and other substitutes.

They both become more concerned about fully living the life they find themselves in than about correcting past wrongs and disappointments.

Conclusion

A couple's happiness depends on the convergence between principles of how to be intimate partners and the unique qualities and story of each individual relationship. Every effective therapist offers couples the opportunity for a new perspective about their predicaments as well as their strengths. The more each member feels understood and accepted, the more they are empowered to find their own paths to intimacy as well as problem resolution.

There are rich resources from research and empirically validated models of couple therapy that can deepen the impact and widen the opportunities of every client encounter. The wise therapist stays in closer contact with clients' experience rather than any pre-existing ideas of what will be helpful.

Chapter 6 focuses on the relevance of a person-centred approach with therapy for gay and lesbian couples, as well as the challenges and opportunities faced by same-sex couples and their therapists.

6

Person-Centred Therapy with Gay and Lesbian Couples

This chapter re-emphasizes a core idea of the person-centred approach: understand each couple on their own terms and work towards goals as they define them. The chapter discusses the person-centred core conditions in relation to couples who, more than others, have to create the own norms and roles. Although many ideas are relevant to all sexual minorities – transgender and bisexual couples, for example – we will focus here on gay and lesbian couples. The chapter includes discussion of themes in the literature about same-sex couples as well as a summary of John Gottman's 12-year research comparing gay and straight couples.

The chapter examines the phenomena of homophobia and heterosexism and their effects on the social, legal, familial, educational, religious and child-related environment of a couple. I offer a case example of an individual client's gradual release from the homophobic assumptions of his family of origin. Two case descriptions illustrate the ways in which therapy with gay and lesbian couples is similar as well as different from that of cross-sex couples. Another case illustrates the therapist's role in facilitating the coming-out process with younger clients and their families. Finally, I discuss work with parents distressed by the sexual orientation of their adult children.

The Not Knowing Position with Couples

A person-centred therapist does not know and therefore has to learn the unique story of each couple they see. A straight therapist is in a learning position with a gay, lesbian, transgender or bisexual couple: they cannot presume to know what this couple is troubled by or how they will resolve that trouble. This, of course, is how it should be for a gay therapist with a straight couple or a straight therapist with a straight couple or a gay therapist with a gay couple!

Person-Centred Core Conditions and Same-Sex Couples

I discuss the six conditions of the person-centred approach once again, because they create a dynamic framework that is particularly relevant in therapy for couples who live lives different from those of couples in the dominant culture.

1. *Psychological contact.* 'In any therapy, there is a period of testing whether the therapist can be patient, nonjudgmental, responsive and worthy of trust ... It is the therapist's responsibility to create opportunities to let clients know that coming out will be met with acceptance and equanimity and that news about sexual orientation will be neither discomforting or unwelcome to the therapist' (Bernstein 2000: 449). The therapist meets each client as they arrive with readiness for the encounter on the clients' terms. The clients may need to know the therapist's level of comfort with their sexuality or, if they are there by referral, may take it for granted. The therapist cannot assume whether the clients are in therapy because of a need unique to their sexuality or about a problem any couple would be likely to have.

2. *Client incongruence.* The clients are in therapy for their distress due to a perceived split between who they are and what their relationship is and what they feel they *should* be. Like all couples, they are comfortable with some areas of incongruence in self or other and distressed about others. Like all couples, they respond best to a therapist with a widely embracing acceptance of people as they are and curiosity about what they want to become. For example, a couple's level of sexual activity is congruent or not with their own and their partner's current expectations, not with the therapist's.

3. *Therapist congruence.* Clients value acceptance and understanding only from therapists who are authentic and comfortable in their own skin – who 'are integrated' (Rogers 1957). Therapists who are helpful to any couple are at home with that couple's sexuality, and are secure enough to move beyond their own life experience to put themselves in another's shoes without patronizing claims to understand what they don't, in fact, understand. If the clients challenge

them because of perceived judgement or assumptions, they are non-defensive and open about their reactions and intentions. All clients, especially those in oppressed minorities, can take a therapist's unease as their responsibility if the therapist does not own their own thoughts and feelings or if if their attention is distracted by anxiety. For example, a therapist may be reminded of frustration in their own significant relationship that clients could interpret as disapproval of themselves.

4. *Therapist unconditional acceptance of clients.* The effects of homophobia and heterosexism (see below) are a daily reality for every gay and lesbian couple. Only a therapist who is able to embrace every aspect of the couple's life completely can be of use in facilitating growth and problem solving. A therapist is an ally (Boyd et al. 2000) for every client and must particularly be so for members of an oppressed and scapegoated minority. An ally not only unconditionally accepts the client as they are, but is also educated in the myriad ways in which clients are not accepted, rejected or persecuted, as well as making it their business to know about and stand against all forms of oppression.

5. *Therapist understanding of clients' internal frame of reference – empathy.* Therapists attempt to put themselves in their clients' shoes. They educate themselves about the conditions of their clients' lives; they access the emotions they would feel if in their clients' world; suspend their own experience in favour of their clients; and, especially, listen with curiosity, concentration, imagination and willingness to be corrected to their clients' self-disclosure. For example, a therapist with or without children can listen to what it is like to be a parent whose parenthood is not only not supported but also even attacked by dominant-culture parents.

6. *Client perception of therapist attitude.* A member of a dominant culture must be open and not defensive about how clients receive their intended empathy, acceptance and realness. Trust is often an issue for a member of an oppressed culture. Empathy is never an established fact, but is always a sought-after condition. The therapist must seek feedback, especially if a client becomes more quiet or guarded after an exchange with the therapist. Freedom to tell a non-defensive therapist when they unconsciously seem to judge or reject can have a healing effect on clients who have felt forced to be silent in the face of an oppressive culture.

Gay and Lesbian Couples: The Research of Gottman and Levenson

Gottman and Levenson have data from 12 years' research on gay and lesbian couples, including comparisons with cross-sex couples (Gottman et al. 2003).Gottman's findings reflect earlier studies (Blumstein and Schwartz 1983; Kurdek 1998). His view is that 'Overall, relationship satisfaction and quality are about the same across all couple types'; and that 'Gay and lesbian couples, like straight couples, deal with every day ups-and downs of close relationships' (Gottman 2009). Gottman also points out that all those ups and downs take place in a context that includes 'isolation, prejudice and other unique social barriers'.

Among other findings of the Gottman and Levenson studies are these:

- Gay and lesbian couples 'are more upbeat in the face of conflict'. Humour and affection do not necessarily disappear at times of trouble in ways that they can with straight couples.
- Gay and lesbian couples use less controlling, domineering and fear-related tactics during conflict: 'fairness and power-sharing between partners is more important and more common in gay and lesbian relationships than in straight ones' (Gottman 2009).
- 'Unhappy gay and lesbian couples tend to show low levels of "physiological arousal."' This is just the reverse for straight couples, who get very upset during conflict and have trouble calming down. Gottman's studies show that straight couples with high emotionality are at greater risk of separation. In gay and lesbian couples, reduced emotional reactions are more predictive of readiness to separate.
- 'Gay men need to be especially careful to avoid negativity in conflict.' Gottman's reasoning here is that after hurt or perceived attack, gay men are less likely to initiate the 'repair work' that straight and lesbian couples (i.e. those with females) find important (and research finds essential) in maintaining happy, lasting relationships.

Person-Centred Self-Awareness

Self-awareness and openness are important outcomes of person-centred training. In most programmes, therapists spend many hours in large and small groups in which personal sharing is encouraged. Therapists explore many of the themes that clients bring to therapy: family-of-origin experience, social history, spirituality, temperament and success, and failure in work and relationships. Trainees are free to share their sexual orientation and experience – gay, lesbian, bisexual and straight – in a non-judgemental atmosphere is which each person is accepted and encouraged in their own path of intimate love.

It is characteristic of an approach in which congruence is highlighted that acceptance of another person's sexuality is manifested not just in external practices but also in internal attitude. The therapist is not 'portraying' (Mearns and Thorne 1988) non-judgemental interest and encouragement of sexuality different from their own, but has developed or strengthened the attitude that everyone has their own orientation and their own practices.

Homophobia and Heterosexism: External and Internalized

Like racism, homophobia affects all aspects of individual and social life. *Homophobia* is a complex of cognitions and feelings centred on rejection of those who have sexual feelings towards members of their own gender. This complex takes many forms: internally it means that any person, identified as gay or straight, can be uncomfortable with same-sex attraction. This experience can be rejected first in oneself and then in others. Readers may themselves reflect on their own learned attitudes towards gay and lesbian feelings in themselves and their developed and developing perceptions of those who live with this orientation. Among other things, homophobia is a process of projection of unwanted and rejected sides of a person onto another group that is seen as less worthy, damaged, unacceptable and the cause of trouble, independent of their true nature.

I recently saw television advertisements in support of a law restricting gay marriage that emphasized the harm being raised without a father might mean for a little boy. The little boy in the ad had no father in his life, a circumstance that is usually the result of a heterosexual father acting as if separation from their female partner absolves them from responsibility for involvement with their children. Gay relationships, absolutely irrelevant to the boy's abandonment by his father, were the implied cause of his predicament.

Heterosexism refers, among other things, to a worldview and use of language that implicitly assume that heterosexuality is normal and normative (Armstrong, personal communication). Male/female pairings are discussed as the ordinary form of couplehood and parenthood and the privileged and, in some places, only legally recognized form of partnership. Often unconsciously, members of this majority group act as if their relationship is the only way of being, forcing invisibility and sometimes shame on minority couples. Gays and lesbians live every day with language that labels their way of life marginal at best and at times rejected.

Homophobia, of course, has negative effects on straight people. Fear of being different from gender expectations robs boys and girls of the ability to enjoy things that are often associated with the other gender. Members of straight couples can become caught in role expectations that keep them from being responsive to the evolution of their family needs. For example, a man said to his therapist, 'I never thought I would have to worry about process', referring to the recently discovered need for his wife and he to discuss the patterns of their fights. Men in heterosexual relationships can have expectations that their wife will always bring up important topics for discussion and are blind-sided when she cuts them off with a resentment that has built too high for a chance of meeting. Women may adopt a role that constricts them or, most commonly, burdens them with responsibility and feel hopeless about reaching their partner.

Case Example 6.1: Release from Homophobia

Individual therapy with Stephen included the reauthoring (White 2007) of the story of his family of origin. Therapy that was centred around Stephen's re-evaluating of his life growing up with his mother, father and brother was most important for his moving beyond depression and chronic fear. Client-centred listening was central, as well as discussion of homophobia as a force that operated not only on the client but on all the significant people in his life. Awareness of the ways in which homophobia can affect every aspect of self-perception allowed Stephen to separate his own sense of self from all the explicit and implied messages that there was something wrong with him:

● His father was 'disappointed and distant from him'. When he failed to be interested in the sports and outdoor activities that were important to his father and brother, he was at first forced to participate, then left alone. (Note: many gay men are highly interested in sports and outdoor activities.) 'It was not seen as wrong or bad that my father was uninvolved with me. It was just the way it was: what I deserved.'

- His mother was 'worried' about him. He 'always had the idea that she talked about me – that there was something wrong with me', but that was not made explicit.
- His parents forced him year after year to belong to a boy-scout troop that he hated, where he had difficulty making friends and was sometimes bullied.
- He had few friends and the one friend he had was someone his mother told him he should spend less time with, though she did not specify why.
- He was 'sent' to a psychiatrist for reasons that were never made clear. He does not remember what they talked about, but he did not like it. (Being 'sent' to a therapist who is seeing you for reasons known to your parents could not be more different from a therapeutic relationship that you seek out for your own self-directed learning, growth and liberation.)
- When older and clearly aware of his gay orientation, he attended a church that, considered 'compassionate' to gay congregants, was actively rejecting his sexuality and forbidding its expression while 'accepting' him. In this church that encouraged therapeutic approaches to change his sexual orientation (considered unethical by professional organizations in both the UK and the US), mockery of some of his mannerisms and of his sexuality was tolerated if not encouraged.

In therapy, awareness of the role that homophobia played in his life created space for his self-acceptance and increasing liberation from his childhood self-concept. It also gave him the opportunity to have some understanding of who his parents were in relationship to him. Homophobia kept his mother from enjoying his unique gifts, relaxing with him, being confident in his ability to have a happy and successful life. It prevented her from appreciating and accepting herself as the mother of a gifted and likeable son who had nothing wrong that she needed to fix. Much of his childhood suffering easily made sense to him once homophobia's daily impact was factored in. Activities such as his boy-scout troop were never about him and what was good for him, but were symbols of fear and desperate attempts to change what could not and should not be changed. His father, whose perhaps insecure sense of who he was led him to accept only those traits in his son that symbolized his version of masculinity, could be seen as lost and wrong rather than as a person reacting as a father in any legitimate way.

Stephen was able to see that his own qualities of gentleness, openness and his artistic abilities were elements to be celebrated and cultivated rather than to be overcome or, at best, tolerated. He realized that he had qualities of courage, persistence, determination and other strengths that were overlooked or seen as not good enough, rather than as natural parts of a rich and interesting personality. In fact, despite the burdens imposed by homophobia, he was able to live a more healthy, successful, constructive adult life than his father or brother. Realizing the ways in which fear had dominated his parents' view of him and robbed his daily life of much of its pleasure allowed him accept himself with gratitude as the person he was and always could have been.

In the present, Stephen enjoys and takes pride in who he is. Exploration of the ways in which homophobia and heterosexism subtly and explicitly controlled many aspects of his growing up has affirmed his resiliency: he managed to grow, learn and become social under the most adverse conditions. There is a kind of joy in his living – the way a person who had once lived in a totalitarian regime might feel finding themselves in a democracy. Stephen continues to come for widely spaced therapy sessions; most of our work is concerned with the present troubles of work and relationships that any person might have. Sometimes, however, feelings or external troubles with friends and co-workers can be related to homophobia that, identified in Stephen's inner world, lurks in many situations in his outer world.

Same and Different

Rule number one: you must forget that a couple is same-sex; they are the same as any other couple. Rule number two: you must never forget that a couple is same sex; they have unique individual and social experiences that a straight therapist can never fully understand (paraphrase of a Pat Parker poem, Parker 2000; Falicov 2003). Bepco and Johnson (2000) describe 'two realities':

The first is the universal reality of ordinary human beings struggling together to create intimate bonds that allow both individual freedom and family cohesion. The second is the particular reality of societal prejudice: at any moment, a gay or lesbian family can become the object of hate or derision that powerfully affects self-esteem and the level of stress within the family. Being able to hold both of these realities is primary to intervening effectively with any oppressed group ... They can be exquisitely attuned to any uninformed or judgmental attitude.

One of many advantages of life in same-sex couples is that therapists would hesitate to impose their idea of what a relationship should be for a couple who are not bound by centuries of traditional advice about gender-determined roles. Susan Johnson has written that same-sex couples may have an advantage in committed relationships because, not having rigidly defined gender roles, they are free to adapt to their situations as is effective and as they are inclined, rather than attempting to live a stereotype (Johnson and LeBow 2000). Shernoff (2006) has written and my colleague Jamey Collins (personal communication) has commented that heterosexual expectations of monogamy and fidelity may be differently defined in same-sex relationships.

As in all effective couple work, the therapist must discover the clients' own troubles and goals as well as their strengths and advantages. Therapists wishing to be allies listen to their clients' descriptions of life as a minority. I will list a few conditions, with which readers may be familiar in some but thankfully not all countries, for the purpose of emphasizing the oppression that is always in the background for some minority couples:

- Governmental laws affecting financial and fiduciary matters between couples including, in some jurisdictions, limiting of visits with hospitalized partners and children.
- Exclusion from end-of-life or medical decision making for one's life partner.
- Ambiguous and easily threatened custody of one's biological children (to a straight ex-partner) and biological children of one's partner, planned and raised together.
- Restrictions on adoption of children.
- Threats to one's job or membership of the armed forces.
- Exclusion from one's preferred religious affiliation except by willingness to hide, change or renounce one's sexual orientation or one's partner.

- Always and everywhere, the possibility of insult, rejection and physical danger because of one's sexual orientation.

There is a growing literature on gay and lesbian relationships (Bepco and Johnson 2000). Green et al. (1996) and others (Laird 2000) point out the ways in which heterosexist assumptions can affect the most well intentioned of therapists. For example, the fact that same-sex couples consist of two women or two men has led to assumptions that those relationships would feature problems of disengagement in a gay male couple and fusion or enmeshment in a lesbian couple. In one study, Green et al. (1996) 'found, contrary to the stereotypes, that the gay male couples in their sample had higher ratings of couple cohesion than did heterosexual couples'. Similarly, their research indicated that what had been called 'fusion or over-closeness between lesbians is actually experienced by most lesbian couples as a satisfying, high degree of cohesiveness and connections'.

Gender, of course, is complex and each couple may have features that fit a profile as well as abilities and coping skills that transcend expected patterns. Gender, Laird (2000) reminds us, can be about cultural expectations and so-called normal socialization. It can also represent the experience of becoming alientated from one's gender by internalized messages of unacceptable differentness. Bepco and Johnson (2000) recommend the clinical practice of a 'post-modern therapist which resembles the ethnographic stance of an anthropologist seeking to learn more about his/her cultural informants from them'. Laird (2000) recommends what she calls an 'informed not-knowing'. A person-centred approach that respects the clients' 'locus of evaluation', as discussed in Chapter 1, and forms a therapy based on listening and client self-direction allows a true meeting with couples who are finding their own experience separate from dominant cultural narratives.

As with all couples, the therapist is a facilitator working with couples' own descriptions of their distress towards their own identified place of relief and harmony. The more therapists educate themselves, the less the couple has to expend energy to explain their situation in general terms. The therapist is then free to focus on the particular frustrations and goals of each unique couple. Each of the three cases described below shows a therapy that seeks both to engage with each couple or family on their own terms, and also to show awareness of the effects that homophobia and heterosexism have on the clients' lives.

Case Example 6.2: Therapy with a Gay Male Couple

Phil and Garry centred around a pursuer/distancer dynamic (see Chapter 3) in which the more Phil sought time alone, the more, despite his intentions, Garry complained and demanded more time together. Phil was in a period of struggle in his own life. Disappointed in career, troubled by money problems, he was unhappy with himself and the way his life was turning out. The couple came to therapy because their relationship had turned into a series of frustrating fights that left Phil depressed and shut down and Garry hurt, guilty and lonely.

Speaker/listener (see Chapter 5) sessions were helpful. This process allowed both people to speak their mind without having the other person immediately refute them. Building on this in other sessions, the therapist took an active role as translator. Garry did feel alone and Phil's habit of staying up late watching television rather than coming to bed left him confused and frustrated. Phil, feeling loss of control in his career and financial issues, needed to be in charge of his bedtime and where he slept. Both were able to understand the other's position while retaining the right to decide on their own behaviour.

In some sessions, each member of the couple was able to listen to the other's struggles and needs independent of the relationship. Like many people in love, Garry had let go of many of the interests and friendships he had in order to spend more time with Phil. When Phil needed more time alone, Garry felt stranded without friend and focus and would become 'needy' in a way that he disliked as much Phil did.

Some of Phil's need for time alone and television watching was the result of his own depression rather than an effect of the relationship. He had stopped school too early and was unhappy with the jobs available to him. (Low self-esteem or other effects of homophobia may have influenced decision making when school may have been more easy, but this was not presented as a problem to explore in the couple therapy.) More important than the relationship was his decision about his work plan: how would he get the training he needed for the work he wanted? The more he focused on career, the less depressed he was.

Garry needed to recover his own sense of self by restoring some of the friendships and activities that preceded his relationship with Phil. The more active he was, the less demanding he was. Both men saw the therapy as an opportunity to speak about what was important to them rather than becoming opponents unwilling to listen.

For this couple and some, but by no means all, couples in their twenties and thirties, homophobia was a less urgent issue. Both men were accepted as gay by their families, who were also welcoming to their partners. Both had come out in their teens, were comfortable in their identity as gay males and had friendships with straight as well as gay women and men; they were out in their workplaces without negative effects. Family rejection, work unavailability, difficulty in the coming-out process or a sense of being restricted to a 'gay enclave' could in other circumstances create an entirely different story and require a different therapy (Chou, personal communication).

The practice of empathy, seeking to know each person's internal frame of reference, builds trust in all couples, but is especially important with clients who have been the object of majority assumptions, labelling and prejudice. Every couple is both different from all others and the same.

Recently, a lesbian therapist in-training asked how she could possibly ever see a straight couple: she would not know enough about their experience, especially that of the male. I was reminded of the case I describe next and told her that she could be more effective in some ways because she would have to concentrate on learning his story from him, rather than acting as if she already knew it. This trainee was also concerned that she would side with the female against the male. In practice, every therapist has to deal with at least a small judgement in favour of one member of a couple; a condition from which only empathy can give release.

Case Example 6.3: Therapy with a Lesbian Couple

Julia and Sue came to therapy during a crisis. The male therapist was interested in why they had called him rather than a lesbian or another female therapist. They assured him that they had been referred to him and, in effect, said they knew what they were doing! One thing I resolved at that moment, which may seem obvious to readers, is that if a couple have chosen you as their therapist, whether you share their gender or orientation, they need you to commit to them with all your confidence and skill. If they want you to facilitate, facilitate! Leave it to them to decide you are not right for them.

What did the therapist do? He listened and translated and, especially, normalized. The current issue was the effects of Sue's chronic pain caused by arthritis. The pain led her to not participate in social or physical activities in a way that has significantly changed their relationship. It made her easily irritated and sometimes to prefer silence to conversation. Her partner alternated sympathy and concern with impatience and feeling threatened by the absence of the more intense social contact she needed. They were kind and considerate and easy with one another by habit, but their new differences had worn confidence and comfort thin and unexpected 'fights' emerged in which each felt misunderstood and uncared for. Long before the arthritis flare-up, the couple had to make frequent adjustments about Julia's extraversion and family involvement and Sue's introversion and need to be alone or just with Julia.

Much of the change they sought in therapy had taken place already since they made the appointment (Berg and Miller 1992). They had decided to talk with each other – only this time to practise listening rather than defending or challenging. Each one had put forward her point of view clearly and had been heard on her own terms. As a result, Sue had felt more closeness and the return not of passion, but of its possibility. Julia had learned that Sue's withdrawal and seeming to turn more to friends than her partner were not about not loving Julia, but reflected a need for withdrawal from anyone and anything that has expectations of her.

As a therapist, I facilitated their gradual addressing of remarks to one another: 'Looks like there is something here you really want Sue to understand.' 'Sue, what do you think is at the heart of what Julia is saying?' (See Wile 1993 on 'trying to get something across'.)

I offered this formulation to facilitate a look at their troubles in which no one was in the wrong – 'It seems for many couples there are six possibilities about doing things together vs apart:

- 'You come with me even though you don't want to.'
- 'You stay home and are angry at me for being out without you.'
- 'I stay home with you even though I want to go out.'
- 'I go out sometimes and enjoy myself while you feel glad to be home alone.'
- 'I sometimes stay in because you want me to and we both feel good about that.'
- 'You come out with me sometimes at a time and in a way that you can enjoy.'

This type of formulation offers clients a kind of multiple choice that allows them to feel that their struggles are part of the path that many other couples take in learning how to live together. The couple feel known. If the relationship is well developed, they can correct it and describe other elements that I have left out.

I offered this couple the chance to use speaker/listener. I explained the approach to them and said that many other couples used it. They said that they didn't feel quite ready for it. 'Too vulnerable,' said Julia. In fact, they were both good speakers and good listeners in the therapy.

As I always do, I asked about their 'physical relationship'. (This coy formulation is partly a result of my own shyness and partly taught me by a hundred couples who use the words 'our intimacy' or 'our physical relationship' to bring up the topic of sex. They prefer it to 'How's your sex life?' – a phrasing that others may be able to achieve but I can't.) I asked the couple, as I almost always do, whether or how their sex life had survived all their physical and emotional difficulty. As almost always happens with couples, they readily answered the question. One of them talked about the loss of desire because of her pain and tiredness; the other of alternating between understanding and also being frustrated by the suspension of their sexual contact. Almost every couple I have met wants some understanding of their sex life to be part of the therapy. Even if they are not ready to address it, they need a therapist who knows and understands how it is with them. To ask about sex and listen with understanding normalizes an area in which many couples feel not very normal.

When therapists show willingness and ability to talk on their terms about sex in a gay/lesbian relationship, they empower the clients to decide for themselves how much they want to talk about it. The therapist signals willingness to take on whatever the clients need. Not to bring up sex leaves the clients uncertain about what is permitted or, at worst, what is forbidden to be discussed. It should never be taken for granted that if a couple improves their relationship, their sex life will also improve automatically. The opposite is true (Treadway 2008).

The brief therapy with Julia and Sue was an opportunity for issues that created tension and stagnancy to be released and become conversation.

An important part of a family therapist's work is assisting families in dealing with a member's sexual orientation. This is becoming easier in western culture as homophobia all too gradually recedes from legal and psychological credibility, although it remains an issue.

Case Example 6.4, despite its relatively happy ending, gives a picture of the loneliness, fear and need for secrecy from which numerous young people suffer in families in which heterosexuality is assumed.

Case Example 6.4: Therapy with an Adolescent Male and His Mother

Darrell and his mother Jeanne came to therapy. Darrell was very isolated during his summer vacation. He had had a lot of kids 'talking about him', avoiding him and sometimes threatening him, because he had been involved with a girl who had a boyfriend already who was jealous of him. His school had become intolerable to Darrell and his mother was willing to transfer him to another school, but wanted Darrell to see a therapist about the trouble he had making friends and the impulsivity that caused him to be rejected at his current school. I listened to the talk of this concerned parent and her son and made an offer to 'check in' with each of them individually as well. Darrell quickly agreed with this idea.

When we were alone, Darrell quickly said, 'There is no trouble with a girl. I am gay and my mother doesn't know it. I want to go to this other school where I have more friends and where kids know I am gay and are OK with it.' I asked him what I could do to help and was told that he wanted someone there when he told his mother. He didn't feel ready to do so in this session, but wanted to do it in the next. We talked about how he would tell her and what the issues might be for her. He thought she would be 'OK with it' but that she might have trouble dealing with his stepfather and stepbrother about it. He particularly wanted me to see his mother individually after he told her so that she could talk about her reactions without him 'having to listen to it'.

The next session, when I found Darrell and Jeanne in the waiting room, I invited Darrell to come in alone for a 'check-in' to see what he wanted from the session. 'Oh it's OK, I already told her,' he said casually. I saw them both together and found that they were handling things well. Jeanne showed no conscious homophobia and the remaining three or four sessions with her and her son were spent on other concerns: what to do with free time; Darrell's school performance; money issues; and issues with Darrell's biological father, who had just turned up in town after two years of no contact. Jeanne's problems were those common to a mother of a son with a stepfather who is ambivalent towards her child and a biological father who is unreliable and uninvolved. Soon after, Darrell had a boyfriend and she was concerned about their being sexually active. In this she shared the dilemma of many parents and many teenagers: managing desire, safety and reason – parents who want kids to go slow and kids are eager for life and sexual experience. This was an issue they seemed to work on with the same amount of trouble and agreement that most parents and teenagers are able to manage.

'Gay people may have problems but who they love is not one of them' (Salama and Chou 2009). Once Darrell felt free to be himself around his mother, he had ample strength and presence to handle other people in his life. He offered his stepbrother little sympathy in his adjustment: 'Look, it's the same as you feel only for me it's boys not girls!'

Parents of Gay and Lesbian Children: Empathy and Advocacy

Parents sometimes come to therapy by themselves to express their desire to change their children's sexual orientation. Two things are important for a therapist. The first, as always, is listening to clients' problems and understanding their frame of reference. Many parents grew up with the thoughts that first, being gay or lesbian was a terrible fate for their children; and second, that they were supposed to do something about it. Allowing parents to talk in a non-judgemental atmosphere gradually reveals to them that they can do nothing about their children's sexuality, except exert the normal and gradually reduced control any parent has over their children's comings and goings.

Particularly challenging are thoughts about homosexuality that arise from rigid religious convictions. I never argue with a parent over their feelings about the wrongness of homosexual acts. A lecture from someone perceived as a liberal who knows better accomplishes nothing. I am not a therapist if I don't listen to parents' heart-felt fears and values with understanding and without judgement. I also trust in the natural process of their children's development and the parents' own actualizing tendency (see Chapter 1). Their children are seeking a way to be sexual beings *and* to be in contact with their parents. The parents are learning to balance their own disappointment in their children's different sexual orientation with their sometimes overlooked unconditional bond with them.

I do offer questions that have to do with their control and power over their children. In what way are their children's sexual feelings a choice? How did they react in their own teen or young adult years to their parents' attempts to control whom they love? What is their role in relation to their children's feelings and decisions? What is in a parent's power and what is not? It is important to note that these questions are asked with expectation of dialogue, not challenge. If I am feeling judgemental or urgent to correct my clients, I should keep my thoughts to myself. Many clients have thought of these questions or are searching for a way to look at their situation that allows more flexibility with their children. If the client is offended by the questions, which has not yet happened to me, the therapist can listen empathically to their reasons for distress. (See Chapter 3 on a congruent approach to non-defensiveness.)

There are two educational efforts that I make. I refer parents to and give out printed material from the websites of the American Psychiatric Association and the Royal College of Psychiatry. Most professional websites present an unequivocal position that homosexuality is not a choice and leads to a lifestyle with no detriments, except for rejection and mistreatment by those who are prejudiced against this orientation – including parents and other family members. While I listen to families struggle about their children's orientation, I feel ethically obligated to eliminate assumptions that there is any scientific or professional support for the practice of homophobia. At the same time, I am an ally for people finding their way in a world in which they have little preparation to live.

Case Example 6.5: Individual Therapy for a Distressed Father

Bill told me the story of his great love and support for his bright, attractive youngest daughter, Sara. Since the middle of her university years, she had been 'changed' by her relationship with Carolyn, who was lesbian. More and more involved with Carolyn, Sara became less and less involved with her parents when they attempted to ask her to stop seeing Carolyn. It seemed clear that Sara is living in a lesbian relationship, but Bill could not quite bring himself to admit it. He was in great distress. His religion and particular church and minister advocated using rejection as a way to force children to give up non-heterosexual lifestyles. 'You can always love her, but just let her know that she is always welcome alone at your house, but you cannot go to her house as long as that other person lives there,' was the advice of their minister and the position of his wife.

I listened to Bill for four sessions. I understood his dilemma: he could not have full participation in his church and still accept his daughter completely. Openness to his daughter's partner could cause a rift with his wife. Our sessions allowed expression of the importance of his daughter to him; of his understanding that she might herself be longing to spend more time with her parents; of his desire to find a way to be closer to her. I did not become an advocate for him to change his religion. It was important that I seek to understand his position just as it was and accept him as a loving man with an impossible dilemma. In order to be congruent, I did raise questions that included:

● What would he do if his parents forbade him to be with the woman who became his wife?
● Would his religion want him to withhold love for his daughter for any reason?

These questions could only be raised with respect and without my assuming that there could be only one answer to them.

I also offered my sense of what his daughter might feel in response to things he and his wife said and did. I invited him to reflect on the reasons why she might have said or done some of the things he found hurtful. I also encouraged his reflection on the meaning of his daughter's recent outreach and willingness to see more of his wife and him. At the end of our sessions, he was not able to see his way clear to reach out to his daughter's partner, though he implied that he would be more likely to if his wife were willing. (She did not attend any sessions, though I made it clear she would be welcome.) He had found more ways to have more contact with his daughter, reported that he felt 80 per cent better about the chance they could work things out and said, 'I guess my main job is to love her unconditionally.' 'That's what I think my job is with my daughters,' I replied. 'Sometimes I have found it difficult.'

Conclusion

All person-centred therapy is directed by clients' unique goals and perceptions of their difficulties. Gay and lesbian couples, like all couples, need therapists who listen, don't make assumptions and accept them unconditionally. At the same time, the more the therapist is willing to understand the conditions in which a couple live, particularly the multiple impacts that homophobia and heterosexism have on clients' lives, the more the therapist is culturally prepared to be an ally in the clients' world. Person-centred therapists can facilitate clients' individual differentiation from homophobic family systems. They can also help parents torn between their love for their children and their religious and political belief systems to find a way to be both true to themselves and true to their children.

Change in parents' attitude, as a key to their alliance with their children and the therapist's practice of multi-directional partiality in understanding predicaments of more than one generation, is an important theme in the next chapter. In Chapter 7, we will discuss a person-centred approach to therapy with families with children and adolescents.

7
Family Therapy with Children and Adolescents

'We are having another family therapy meeting with Jeff and his therapist,' said my friend, Jack, about his 18-year-old son. 'Oh yeah?' I asked. 'What do you think of that?' 'I don't know,' he said, without a trace of enthusiasm. 'I guess I'm going to have to look at things from another point of view.' I knew what he meant: family therapy with my oldest daughter was good for us all, but meant learning about my own blind spots and the unwelcome impact of some of my well-intended words and actions. Individual therapy is easier: the therapist accepts you and the only person you have to learn from is yourself – at your own pace! A relationship therapist offers empathy to each person in the presence of family members who may prefer that others be corrected rather than understood. The therapist makes sense out of their disappointment without joining in it. Family therapy is, in part, the sorting out of the disappointment natural to all human relationships from something wrong that requires action or change.

Family therapy with children and adolescents can be a complete therapy in itself as well as an adjunct therapy for children receiving other services for special needs. In this chapter I present most frequent reasons for family therapy; all have in common the need for family and parental change as well as, and sometimes more important than, change in the individual child. Person-centred therapy for young people makes sure that each voice is heard and validated and that relationships are attended to at least as much as issues of child behaviour or performance. After examples of the effects of a person-centred approach on client attitudes and future adult adjustment of children treated in a person-centred way, I discuss the core conditions in therapy with young people. A case example of brief therapy spread over eight years (two to five sessions at key developmental crises) illustrates the importance of multi-directional partiality – being on the side of everyone at once. The chapter illustrates person-centred reflection in work with children and adolescents and their families. There is a separate section on work with children from highly stressed families. One case example of work with a child's family and another with the family of a late adolescent show the therapist's need to balance individual respect with awareness of evolving roles in family life.

Reasons for Family Therapy with Children and Adolescents

Clients seek therapy for children and adolescents for these reasons among others:

- An incident or incidents at home, school or in the neighbourhood that provokes worry about impulse control, knowledge of right and wrong or safety.
- Under-performance or refusal to attend school or inability or unwillingness to follow rules at school or home.
- Hostility towards parent, stepparent or siblings.
- Anxious, immature or controlling parents have unrealistic and unhelpful expectations. Parents or other adults have conflicting expectations about child behaviour, achievements, residency, custody and values.
- Reaction to a separation, divorce or involvement with a potential stepparent, cohabiting adult, relative or friend and/or their children.
- Reaction to parental conditions such as alcohol or drug abuse, illness, prolonged separation or inability to be a responsible adult.
- Reaction to physical abuse or sexual exploitation by an adult or another child.
- Signs of depression or anxiety shown by withdrawal and avoidance of activities and enthusiasm expected by significant adults.
- Reaction to physical, mental or learning disabilities, illnesses or other conditions, including real or perceived giftedness.
- Something the child does (see all other reasons, except perhaps depression or anxiety) provokes someone to say that the child has Attention Deficit Disorder with Hyperactivity (ADHD).

First, the person-centred family therapist pays attention to the presenting problem as a collaborator with clients. They relate the events of the therapy to that issue while seeking each person's opinion and feelings about the issue. Their priority is listening to each person's point of view throughout the therapy. For example, diagnoses of depression, ADHD or other conditions are the opinions of adults about which a young person's thoughts and feelings must be consulted if any therapy is to take place. Anderson (1997) writes of a mother's letter describing several years of her daughters' failed therapy for anorexia:

> Much too often our daughters have felt that their opinions were not important, that no one was prepared to listen to them and work through them instead of through us [the parents]. It would have cost them, and us, much less pain if more effort had been made trying to influence their own motivation ... Make it easier for their self-respect to grow. (Anderson, 1997: 8)

Second, the therapist is concerned about the relationship between family members independent of the presenting problem. For example, parents of a child with disabilities may spend so much effort and attention on remediation of the child's perceived deficits that little is left for the open-ended, agenda-free experiences that bring joy and closeness to families. Similarly and most commonly, parents, feeling an urgent need to control teenage behaviour and influence adolescent character, may gradually lose the experience of friendship and respect that shapes a lifetime of human connection (Taffel 1991).

Third, thinking systems invites more complex ideas about a family's trouble than the need to 'fix' a young person. Quite often, each of the issues described above may happen simultaneously with one or more of the other issues. A child's behaviour may happen in relation to a parent's behaviour. For example, a child misbehaving at school may be acting in relation to problems between parents that are made more complex by the child's troubles and so on. A non-judgemental therapist offering 'non anxious presence' (Friedman 1991) may allow each person to feel less stress themselves and therefore bring less stress to other family members.

Fourth, person-centred therapy is responsive to effects on the long-term self-concept of clients along with their short-term well-being. Many of our adult clients have had experiences of therapy as teenagers and/or children. For some clients, the experiences were at best irrelevant to them, at worst coercive and shaming. What if they had experienced a truly person-centred childhood family therapy? If so, what would be the effects on them today had they received the following?

- A therapist who 'belonged' to them as much to the other members of the family.
- The attention of an adult whose absolute priority was to listen to them carefully and encourage their parents to listen to them and show understanding of their point of view.
- The experience of seeing their parent or parents in dialogue with a respectful adult about their children's trouble rather than isolated in frustration.
- Reassurance that their problems made sense to another adult and received reassurance that there was a way to talk about feelings without harming anyone.
- A facilitator for their parents rather than the hopeless experience of listening to their parents express blame, doubt, fear or threats to their children or one another.
- The experience of seeing their family accepted with respect and even liking as they were and found that their troubles were like the troubles that many people had.

A wise family therapist may manage to facilitate a healing and growth-producing atmosphere that develops potential and heads off discouragement. An unwise therapist practises as an evaluator and authority who leaves people feeling exposed and shamed. Whatever the experience, therapy as a child and adolescent has an effect on adult self-concept.

In the Mind of a Person-Centred Family Therapist

Thinking like a person-centred family therapist means being aware of the following:

- Each person, however apparently inarticulate, has an explanation of what the trouble is that can be brought into the conversation without refuting another's point of view. The therapist never forgets that there is an inner experience or intention behind every action and word.
- Each moment in a family's life is transitional, though it may seem literally like the end of the world or, at least, like the end of happiness for one or more family members. The therapist sees family life as an evolving process rather than a collection of individuals with set roles and point of view.

- Therefore, each moment in a family's life can be seen in relation to the future of the young people on their way there or to past unresolved issues, carried mostly by the parents. The therapist expects conflicting priorities, values and goals and is at home with clarifying differences as normal rather than destructive. The therapist is aware of people who, though in the role of children and subordinates, will remember the occasion as autonomous, evaluating adults. Similarly, those in the role of parents are themselves former children and future elderly.

- Each family or, certainly, members of the family can need *believable* reassurance that the therapist accepts them and their troubles as those a normal or functional family may have. The therapist is active and vocal, because clients often feel shame and hopelessness about their particular predicaments. If the therapist does not express their thoughts and feelings, the clients may project judgement and disapproval onto them.

- The actualizing tendency, the never-ending unfolding of human development, is at work in the midst of the most discouraging of human predicaments. The therapist does not sell this or preach this, but this point of view informs their questions, commentary and framing of issues.

- The therapist does not impose 'shoulds' on the family, nor expect an idealized way of being. On the other hand, they may relate issues to the usual expectations of family life and milestones.

- The therapist is aware that a young person is either ready or not ready to talk. Clients are not seen silent, shut down, refusing to talk, resistant, unwilling or uncooperative. It is just that the conditions are not ready for them to talk. This is an important application of non-judgemental acceptance. No matter what, the young client is not an opponent of the therapist and, of course, the therapist is never an opponent of the young person.

- The therapist must deal with societal and personal fear when working with teenagers. Violent incidents in schools and elsewhere can make parents, therapists and other people in authority afraid to trust young people and quick to make restrictive diagnoses and referrals. There is, of course, no guarantee that a young person will avoid reckless or dangerous action. A person-centred approach both involves listening to teens and children on their own terms and listening to parents as they reflect on what they can and should control and what belongs to their childen.

- The person-centred approach is a way of being (Rogers 1980; Wood 2008) rather than a collection of techniques. The therapist may use techniques as a way to respond to client goals and predicaments, as long as the techniques do not impose therapist authority or superiority on the system.

Case Example 7.1: Both of You Make Sense to Me

Coralee and Ricky came to therapy because 11-year-old Ricky had shown other children a pocketknife at church Sunday school. The teacher had put together that incident with another in which Ricky was shoving a boy to express reasons for worry about Ricky's tendencies towards aggression. (We also live in a time and a state, Colorado, in which any unusual behaviour can provoke an attitude of fear towards a child; see below.) Ricky was half-Hispanic with an immigrant father who was divorced from his Anglo, soon to be retired nurse mother when he was about 4. His mother had chosen a family therapist to see whether Ricky needed special intervention for potential violence.

The first four visits included sitting with Coralee and a fairly silent Ricky and listening to the family story. Brief individual visits with Ricky included lots of questions about how he spent his time and what he liked and didn't like. A visit was scheduled with his father, along with Ricky and his mother. All seemed comfortable with one another; the bringing of a knife to Sunday school made more sense as his showing off important possessions to friends than as any attempt to harm or intimidate.

The family determined that the therapy was a place where all could talk and be listened to; that the therapist was not diagnosing them in any mysterious way; and that the therapist was comfortable with them as they were. It was most important, perhaps, that each person could talk or not talk, agree or not agree, without having to fear that they or the family would be judged or rejected.

Ricky and his mother came in about once a year during the course of Ricky's teenage years. Ricky gradually began to talk more and sometimes initiated the meetings. A routine was established with which all were comfortable. There would be a brief meeting of the three of us in which, usually, Coralee would explain the main reason for the meeting with Ricky, making brief corrections. Then the therapist would meet with one of them alone, usually Coralee, sometimes Ricky, especially when he had initiated the meeting. The therapist would get that person's story, then listen to the other's point of view in a second individual meeting.

Though Ricky needed more questions to get him started, the therapy became a place in which his story could be told while the therapist translated his mother's side without taking it. The third step would be a meeting that included both of them. Each would make a proposal and get some agreement from the other as well as some disagreement. The therapist would highlight agreements and also help make them more specific. He would also describe what was not agreed on, without implying that that disagreement meant any inadequacy or trouble.

Among the issues discussed over the years were these:

- Ricky's motivation to study and work compared to Coralee's expectations.
- A few brief incidents of Ricky skipping school and lying to cover it up and many instances of skipping homework.
- Ricky's desire to change schools to an easier programme with fewer academic requirements and more extensive outdoor activities.
- Ricky falling in love and Coralee setting restrictions on amount of contact and expressing many concerns about sexuality.
- Ricky's use of money and quitting a job despite accumulated expenses.
- A major incident involving near alcohol poisoning.
- Getting a driving licence; getting a car.
- Chores, loud music, dishes and food in room, chores, loud music, cleanliness, chores, loud music, respect and freedom, freedom and respect. Did I mention chores and loud music? Did I mention Ricky's need for freedom and his mother's need for respect?

A family therapist provided each person with both a chance to be heard and a way to compromise with the other without losing dignity or self-respect. He was also there for reassurance that this small, sometimes isolated family of a woman very different temperamentally from her beloved son could make it together. In effect, the family was asking: 'Are we OK? Do we make sense?' The therapist would not answer such a question, but their talking in the presence of someone calm who liked them both and was not surprised by their troubles gave them encouragement. Usually two or three sessions would be enough before they would stop, until the next obstacle.

When Ricky was 17 an incident occurred that scared both of them. Ricky, much bigger and stronger, blocked Coralee's way to turn down music she found overwhelmingly ugly and loud. Coralee pulled a lamp from a wall and struck him with it. Both were appalled and ashamed. Through his window the therapist watched them walking to his office, 10 feet apart, for a session Ricky had called to schedule. The telling of the story that included Ricky's determination to move out of Coralee's and in with his father was sombre and unpromising. Seen alone, both were animated, revealing a month of accumulating frustrations as well as realization that things were different, and both were perhaps ready for a change in the mother–son structure that they had needed for so long. The result of the session was that they could talk to each other civilly, although how each would handle injured dignity or the question of who was to blame was unresolved.

The next session was as good-humoured, companionable and confident as the previous one was bleak. Ricky's girlfriend's parents had done something awful to Ricky and their daughter. Coralee, along with her ex-husband, had stood up for Ricky with indignation at his accusers and trust in him. This revelation of their truer unity quickly made their scary division fade into the background. The problem was 'dissolved' (Anderson 1997) by conversation.

After this last incident, the therapist hears only the occasional news a friend might receive. Ricky still lives with Coralee while he is in a professional training programme. They are linked by earned affection and respect and of course, in our current times, economic necessity.

Like many of my readers, much of my career was spent in agencies, seeing non-voluntary as well as voluntary clients. As shown in the discussion below, empathy and unconditional positive regard, adapted to clients living with economic and legal pressures as well as relationship predicaments, formed the core requirement of the work.

Therapy in the Public or Voluntary Sectors

What follows are brief reflections on therapy with clients in what William Madsen calls 'multi-stressed families' (2007) in a richly detailed study of work in public agencies. He describes families with fewer resources than those seen in a private practice and includes families who are mandated to therapy due to law enforcement problems or because children have been taken out of the home after neglect, abuse or parental distress. Madsen offers these suggestions, among many others:

- an emphasis on strengths;
- collaborative goal setting;
- keeping the problem on the table without judging;
- representing the client, not the various social agencies that may be involved;
- flexibility over ambiguous motivation, time, place and content of meeting.

He describes family members saying of their therapists: 'The workers were so respectful; I know we gave them a hard time, but they just kept coming back' and 'They were the first professionals who really listened to me.'

Almost 80 years ago Carl Rogers started his career at the Rochester Child Guidance Clinic and worked with the parents of many court-referred and otherwise stressed children. In those days he, as a psychologist, saw parents, as did social workers, while psychiatrists saw children. He recounts that his life and work changed when he realized that his telling parents what to do, in however benevolent a way, was less helpful than listening to clients' own formulation of their problems as well as their way out of them. In his autobiography (Rogers 1967) he describes one woman, to whom he had admitted that their therapy about her son was unsuccessful, asking before she left if he would see her about her own problems. His work changed course completely: 'It began to occur to me that unless I had a need to demonstrate my own cleverness and learning, I would do better to rely upon the client for the direction of movement in the process.'

Acceptance of all family members as they are and a strength-based approach that builds on competence is at the heart of work with families who have negative experiences with social service agencies, schools and law enforcement. Elias Lefferman is the CEO of Vista Del Mar, a large Los Angeles, California agency serving children in residential treatment or foster care because of emotional or behavioural challenges as well as parental disability, addiction, imprisonment or neglect or abuse. In a recent interview, he expressed the following:

- Every child needs to feel connected to their family in order for them to learn and heal. Even if their parents are unable to care for them or for themselves, the child needs to be in whatever contact can be managed and know that their clinician holds their relationship as valuable.
- He employs a 'family finder', whose job includes locating family members for each child, with the goal of having the child meet or in

some way stay connected with their parents, siblings, grandparents, aunts and uncles or whatever person might be available to the child.

- Therapists focus on family members' strengths and positive qualities or histories rather than attempting to control, criticize, exhort or demand. 'Find one thing they can do right,' says Elias. 'That's the one thing the therapist can hang their hat on.' It allows the, often defensive, family to connect with the therapist in a situation that is often seen as oppositional versus collaborative.
- Elias has worked with families of children in distress since the 1970s. Sometimes parents of children don't want help. 'You hear what they are saying [things you can't condone] but you don't disagree [or agree]'; 'I like to ask questions … about the parents and their lives. You call up a father and say you need him to help you, Vista and the family in order to help the child. You ask for help.'
- You embrace the family. The family feels that you want what's best for them. You are never 'smarter than them'. Respect is most important.
- Elias described the work of Israeli colleagues whose work he saw: 'They would study video tapes and find one thing that was positive. For example, they would see a father put his arm around a kid, walking into the session. They would spend the whole session on that: how could it happen that the father would do that? – what could it mean in that moment that the father would do that?' (Lefferman, personal communication). This parallels Michael White's concept of 'unique outcomes' or the art of paying attention to unexpected loving or competent events, as we have seen in Chapter 1 (White and Epston 1990).

In our current decade, an experienced therapist, steeped in the strength-oriented traditions of family therapy, is echoing Rogers' 1930s discoveries. Unconditional positive regard and emphasis on supportive listening on the clients' terms remain key values. Dr Lefferman's approach also emphasizes awareness of systems in a way that Rogers may have been aware of but never wrote about directly. Vista Del Mar promotes the direct physical connection with family members as equally important as any supportive one-on-one or group contact with young clients.

Thinking Like a Family Therapist for Children

The person-centred family therapist for children wants to meet those children in such a way that they feel comfortable, affirmed and worth listening to. All techniques, all goals held by their parents, are subordinate to this primary intention of the therapist. At the same time, the therapist is interested in the parents not just in terms of how they treat their children, but also as persons under pressure trying to fulfil their temporary tasks as guides, protectors, providers, teachers and role models. The therapist may have knowledge that can give relief and perspective to the family, but their primary intention is that the family deserves their interest, their understanding and their support just as they are.

Being person centred does not mean intervening in favour of a different approach to the problem of a child than that taken by their parents. For example, many parents bring children for therapy who are taking medication for Attention Deficit Disorder with Hyperactivity. Other parents may have a more authoritarian way of organizing their household than the therapist or Carl Rogers might choose. For instance, some therapists may take a strong position against medication for or any diagnosis of children (see White 2007 and Law 1997). This therapist listens to each member of the family, supporting each person's point of view and neither imposing nor rejecting diagnoses. In meetings with parents alone, I do seek to understand their rationale for consenting to medication and the history of the child's behaviour with and without medication. A non-judgemental discussion of thinking patterns can allow parents to consider alternative approaches without putting them on the defensive in the face of a therapist's agenda. For example, meeting with the mother and stepfather of 9-year-old Jimmy allowed for the experiment of no medication during the long summer holiday.

Case Example 7.2: Family Therapy with a 9-Year-Old Boy

Therapy with Jimmy took place in three modalities. First, there were family meetings with Jimmy and his mother Bev and stepfather Tom. Those meetings were lively affairs, with the family sometimes moving around the room to different stations labelled 'mad', 'sad', 'glad' and 'afraid' and each person sharing what conditions led to each feeling. Other family meetings went through the times of week and times of day as people shared what was important to them as they lived their lives. Other family meetings included moving around between easy places at school and at home and hard places at those locations. Again, talk was linked to action and the 9-year-old boy was the centre of things without being the object of discussion about him. Experienced family therapists offer child-oriented activities to make the therapy interesting and safe for children.

Second, the therapist met alone with Bev and Tom. They discussed their concerns and plans, their fears and their successes. The therapist facilitated reflection not only on how they handled their responsibilities for Jimmy and his 3-year-old brother, but also how they supported each other. As always, in meetings with parents, the therapist raised questions about how they could enjoy and spend non-purposeful time with their children along with focusing on the behaviour problems that brought them to therapy.

One focus of the meetings with Bev and Tom was their handling of the infrequent availability of Jimmy's father, Jerry, who was in the military and was often unreachable because of long hours, frequent postings out of the area and involvement with his second family, a wife and three very small children. Jimmy loved his father greatly, missed him, worried about him and sometimes expressed anger by refusing tasks at school and home that he usually did well. Among adaptations supported in our meetings were time for Jimmy to express frustration after having to leave his father, more time spent listening to him before expecting him to return to his routine and more open permission for him to call his father when he missed him. When, in fact, Jerry was finally transferred to another state, Jimmy reacted with greater calm and contentment. His parents were more accepting of the normalcy of his sadness and frustration at separation from his father; Jimmy was more satisfied because, with permission for frequent calls and the use of electronic face-to-face visits with his father, he could enjoy his daily life with Bev and Tom without feeling cut off from his dad.

Third, the therapist met with Jimmy and Jerry before Jerry's transfer. The therapist prepared for the meeting with Jerry by writing questions to facilitate the two dealing with the dilemma of Jimmy's maintaining closeness with his adored father despite many deterrent realities. Note: this therapist always prepares questions that seem appropriate to the purpose of the therapy meetings and the family's developmental issues and tasks. The family's agenda has priority over those questions, but they are present to offer support and structure that reduces family pressure to perform. He never knows in advance whether he will offer the questions; he never knows in advance whether the questions, if offered will occupy his clients' attention. Jimmy and Jerry related easily and found ways to collaborate on answers to questions such as: 'What was the time that the two of you had the most fun together?' 'How does each of you think you are alike?' 'How is each of you different?' 'What does each of you need so that you don't miss each other too much when Dad moves?' The session with Jerry and Jimmy served as a kind of ritual of affirming the connection between father and son without denying the frustration of their separation.

Thinking Like a Person-Centred Therapist for Families of Teenagers

Family therapy with adolescents may have these elements:

- Awareness of the developmental tasks not only of the child but of the parents – *all* are adjusting to change in their identity.
- Sorting out the responsibilities that belong to the parents and those that belong to the child.
- The normalizing of the sometimes awkward, sometimes hurtful ways in which young people show their differentiation from their parents.
- Awareness of the co-occurring troubles of adults in a family and those of the child – parents can have trouble in work, love, finances or with their own parents exactly when their child needs most emotional energy.
- Use of outside resources, if necessary, to deal with school problems, substance abuse and disabilities.
- Involvement in and understanding of the pressures of the child's world of friends, electronic systems, dangers mild and severe having to do with driving automobiles, sexuality, self-mutilation and substance-abusing rituals, and the exposure to bullying, group targeting of scapegoats and school inadequacy.
- Awareness of the relationships between parents and their partners and ex-partners and the complexity of co-parenting.
- The problem of child preference for the least involved, least mature parent.

A family therapist for teenagers makes room for change. They make sense out of what seem to be insurmountable difficulties. They give permission for parents to believe that their children have other, more useful qualities than they show in their life at home. In a session with his mother, 15-year-old Alfredo said: 'I'm not good at give and take yet.

Outside the house, I mostly give: to Janey [his girlfriend] and to my friends. In the house, I usually take.' Family therapist Ron Taffel (2005) emphasizes the need for both contact and willingness to back off. In an age of reduced family contact and increased generational separation, parental involvement may feel like parental intrusion, but is a better alternative than parental indifference. The alternative, says Taffel, is that teenagers centre their lives in their 'second family' (Taffel 2001), their friends, who can become the source of their values. Encounters between family members are no less necessary for being awkward and emotionally challenging. Parental involvement and, especially, attempts to find out what their teenagers are doing can produce sometimes angry encounters. Such encounters, Taffel says (2005: 76), are often followed by increased closeness and disclosure by both teenagers and parents.

Case Example 7.3: Family Therapy with an Adolescent

This therapist facilitated a series of, sometimes angry, encounters between Tom, an 18 year old living at home while attending his first year of university, his mother Carolyn and his father Marty. Tom, the oldest of four children, was seen as increasingly sullen and belligerent in his infrequent time at home. When consenting to be part of family activities, he often made his parents regret urging his participation because of unfriendliness, taciturnity and ill-concealed boredom. Family therapy, along with some individual therapy, was initiated by his mother because of the following:

● Tom's increasing refusal to come home at the time indicated by his parents.
● Lots of loud activity when he did come home after everyone else was in bed.
● Two fights with his next youngest brother that scared their mother by their ferocity and the difficulty they had stopping them.
● Withdrawal from competitive model airplane design and competition, in which his father was involved. He had abruptly given up anything to do with airplanes, including his weekly hours of work and frequent days of travel with his father.
● Expressions of fury at both parents, especially his father, when they attempted conversations about their many concerns to do with him.

Individual contact revealed:

- Tom had seen himself as overweight and unpopular until just recently when he lost considerable weight and had better fortune in finding friends who included him and sought him out.
- He saw his parents as 'psycho' in his mother's, to him too frequent, attempts to talk with him about personal matters; and in his father's criticism and attempts to restrict his use of the car they had given him.
- Tom felt that his parents didn't want their kids to grow up; particularly, that they treated him like a kid rather than the adult he was.

In a meeting with his parents, I learned:

- Tom had been the focus of worry throughout his life; although currently a successful student, he had suffered from learning disabilities that involved his mother with him more than her other children.
- His mother and father, like many parents, frustrated each other: she wincing at her husband's tone of voice and critical habit; he frustrated by her softening of agreed sanctions of their son's behaviour.
- They were fearful of Tom's temper; fearful that he would be depressed and hurt himself; worried that he didn't 'feel ready' to live away at university.

A Meeting with the Parents

As with most families with adolescents, I met alone with Tom (and his mobile phone on which he, with apologies, had to receive more than one text message) and also with just Carolyn and Marty. Into one session Tom's parents brought much of the anxiety that parents whose older son has changed greatly often carry. They were also struggling with a paradox: Tom was 'of age' and eloquent on the subject; and he was also at home and dependent on them for everything, including his large new sports utility vehicle. In the middle of a session sorting out what was none of their business and what was theirs to decide, Marty's mobile phone rang. It was their 11-year-old son Robbie reporting that was Tom yelling at him and threatening him because he had asked Tom to turn his music down. Marty immediately stood up to leave and 'get Robbie out of that house'.

I said: 'Hold on. Let's talk about this. Please sit down.' I asked if they really thought that their son was truly a danger to his little brother. If that were true, why weren't they driving Tom to a psychiatric hospital? If their son could not safely be around their other children, wasn't this much more of an emergency than we were acknowledging? Paradoxically, my questions calmed them. They reasoned that they were scared by Tom's anger, but did not expect him to be more trouble than any angry, self-centred older brother.

I went further in my challenge: Why did a boy who could scare a younger brother still have keys to a car his parents owned? Why would there be business as usual, normal privileges, in the presence of unchallenged intimidation? In the rest of the conversation, Marty and Carolyn sorted out where they stood as people and what they would expect of their son as a person. There was no more talk of emergency trips to rescue one son from another or of psychiatric hospitalization. Though it was close to Christmas, I offered to find a time to join them in meeting with their son if they needed me. A phone call later that day from a confident Carolyn let me know that they had had a calming, loving talk with their son and that we all could go ahead and enjoy our Christmas without any emergency.

Reflecting on this encounter, I am aware that I took a stronger position with Tom's parents than I usually do. On the one hand, I challenged their responding to their son as though he were untrustworthy and violent and their sense of having to act as bodyguards between one child and another. On the other hand, I challenged their passivity in the use of powers that reasonably belonged to them. They had plunged headfirst into drastic measures, treating their son as dangerous and out of control, while ignoring more moderate measures that would hold him accountable.

I would have been incongruent if I had not engaged them with these challenges. I also would not be a good therapist if, having entered the situation fully, I did not then step back and defer to their own sense of what felt right to them. Most of the time, I work as a facilitator with clients as they process their own decisions together. Sometimes a less graceful, detached presence is called for to slow down emotional reactivity. We must meet our clients as people as well as professionals (Taffel 2008). Having entered the arena, so to speak, we must also return to our facilitator role to encourage clients to process their experience of our altered role and to restore their sense of control over their own family. The therapist may risk their own emotional reactivity if they do not encourage client reflection on the process. In this case, the encounter ended with the clients taking charge of a more deliberate decision-making process.

A Family Meeting: Sorting Out Rights and Privileges

These challenges, this person-to-person meeting on the edge of feared danger, arose in the context of several meetings with them and with their son and them in which the therapist was an accepting facilitator. In a meeting that followed this by three weeks and occurred after the family had decided that Tom *would* move to the dorms at his university, the therapist facilitated a meeting through varying levels of intensity and closeness.

At first Tom, briskly and with barely concealed irritation, sought to make the meeting about his parents simply allowing him the use of his car with no limitations or expectations. I did not challenge Tom's attitude but reflected back what was most important to him in the moment: control of his car.

His parents wanted to go over the history of Tom's behaviour in the last months, their anger and hurt at his lying to them and their worry about his late-night driving to see a girlfriend who lived many miles away from his dorm. Tom lapsed into demands and lectures about his rights; his parents into their ownership of the car and their concerns about safety and judgement. I named the urgencies each felt: Tom about his rights for autonomy; his parents about their fears. I also summarized what each had said in early sessions. (This is a most important facilitator function. In the heat of emotion, a family frequently loses connection with past understandings or appreciations.) I talked about the developmental tasks they were working on for the whole family: they were, with this oldest son, figuring out how to mix staying close with letting go; support with independence; and especially the right amount of parental involvement.

At one point the parents were determined to take the vehicle from Tom completely and Tom was emphasizing that, over the summer or in the holidays, he would never return home to live with his parents again. I kept naming the issues and acknowledging the difficulty every family has about these decisions. I also shared the feeling of loss and sadness that I felt when I thought that only a year ago Tom and his father were very involved together and his mother was not kept up at night by all the worries she now felt and couldn't get rid of.

A Facilitative Trip to the Bathroom

Tom said that he needed to use the bathroom and asked if that was OK. 'Sure, are you going to come back?' 'Sure.' (One therapist function is to make the purpose of comings and goings explicit. Much family discouragement follows an unannounced, unexplained departure.) Marty and Carolyn calmed themselves and talked about separating the issues of Tom's right to do what he wanted from their safety concerns. A different Tom returned. He admitted that, though he wanted and needed his car, he could understand why they took it from him. Relieved by his more cooperative style, parents offered lifts to see his girlfriend while he was without the car. Tom discussed his questions about whether he was free to come home if he were tense at school. His father, exuberant about the thaw in the room, said that he wanted to keep talking about what it would take for Tom to have his car back. There was even talk about Tom and his dad going to a convention for model airplane craftsmen.

Why did a different Tom return? Family therapy can be an opportunity for clients to access many selves rather than remaining stuck as though lack of cooperation was their own story. Journeying to family therapy expresses an intention to change. Tom stepped out of the fighting teenager and into a calmer, more reasonable self, which immediately melted his scared parents' fear and need for control.

I ended the session by summing up agreements made and facilitating appreciations by each person present for each other person. Family therapy requires engagement in issues that stir strong emotions; it also benefits from the therapist offering reassurance that a family is not just trapped in a struggle but is also managing an important transition. The therapist can keep in mind that a family can be in a seemingly impossible situation while, at the same time, living through their finest hour.

The role of family therapy during life transitions is to allow the feelings behind each person's position to be acknowledged while validating the legitimacy of competing concerns. The therapist also needs a sense of trust that the strong feelings stirred up by issues of respect and freedom can evolve into feelings of closeness and appreciation – and that this cycle can and does repeat until a developmental milestone is passed. The therapist both facilitates each person's expression while asking questions that remind the family of the context that includes past closeness and their future relationship as connected adults.

Conclusion

The core conditions of the person-centred approach facilitate person-to-person meeting in the midst of the troubles that young people experience and the worries and self-doubt that block parents' confidence in and enjoyment of their children. The therapist can hear every voice and validate each point of view while normalizing the unique as well as predictable predicaments that led to the therapy. The therapist can be on each person's side while respecting the many external and internal expectations that influence a family's life. Fear and anger are often overwhelming when the well-being of a child is at stake. The therapist waits for and acknowledges unnoticed or undervalued signs of initiative, strength, imagination and courage.

Chapter 8 highlights opportunities and predicaments in the life of a person-centred relationship therapist and concludes the book with reflections on Carl Rogers as a model and supervisor for couple and family therapists.

8

On Becoming a Person-Centred Couple and Family Therapist

How do you become a person-centred couple and family therapist? How do you re-create an approach that is at once personal to you and your experience and unique to the couple or family who have come to you for help? This chapter will include examples of therapist self-talk, discussion of Carl Rogers and the renewal of person-centred values, attitudes and responses, and reflections on a Carl Rogers interview by a family therapy historian and teacher. It will incorporate reflections on therapist confidence and the resources of experienced and inexperienced therapists. One case example will highlight the qualities of a person-centred approach and another will show a natural systemic change that illustrates the actualizing tendency.

Therapists Do and Should Talk to Themselves

Although I am Irish, I have nothing against positive thinking: that habit of telling yourself and others that things *will* go well; that you *can* do what you need to do; that other people *are worth* trusting. In the winter, when I ski down a hill that for me seems dangerous, curving in a bad-intentioned way near some sullen pine trees, I offer a loud, encouraging lecture to myself and whatever other skiers are nearby. I talk like somebody's eccentric uncle: 'You are doing very well,' I say. 'That's it. Just keep bending your knees and now just put your weight on your right foot. Very good! Not too much longer now. Look ahead of you. That's it! Now just hold. You can stay up right.

Good job!' It gets me down the hill and usually I don't have to switch to the language of acceptance, which might sound like this: 'The trees look more beautiful from the ground. I can move at least one of my legs and one of my arms: that's promising. What do you know? I am still alive.' Similarly, as a therapist getting ready to see clients, it is important to set your own purpose for the session. You are not empowered to solve clients' problems by yourself or to make them feel any different than they do. You are about offering a process that can allow them to reset their own process so that they can find a way to move forward.

I have to talk to myself, even if clients are kept waiting (O'Leary 1999: 67). I cannot show up until I have in some way remembered who I am as a therapist and am ready to find out who they are. If I have met them before, I read notes and take a few notes. I mostly do not use the notes, but they make me remember who these people were when we last met so that I do not confuse them with someone else, literally and metaphorically. (I don't want to mistakenly think that a grandmother lives with them; I also don't want to forget their expressed and unexpressed wishes, their stated and unstated causes of distress or where we left off last session.)

I sometimes listen to Carl Rogers in memory or in his 15 books or hundreds of articles. Thinking about Rogers makes me at once calmer and more intensely ready to move towards meeting the clients in my waiting room. I might sometimes read something like this reflection by Rogers:

> This book is about me, as I sit there with that client, facing him, participating in that struggle as deeply and sensitively as I am able. It is about me as I try to perceive his experience, and the meaning and the feeling and the taste and the flavor that it has for him. It is about me as I bemoan my very human fallibility in understanding that client, and the occasional failures to see life as it appears to him … It is about both the client and me as we regard with wonder the potent and orderly forces which are evident in this whole experience, forces which seem deeply rooted in the universe as a whole. (Kirschenbaum and Henderson 1990: 3–4)

Inspired by this, I wrote the following yesterday that more formally reflects notes that I have written in my journal before beginning a session:

This book is about me as I try to meet each couple or family with attention and trust. It is about me as I try to let my knowledge and experience be present but in the background of my seeking to understand clients on their own terms. It is about me as I seek to be confident in this process without being over eager and trying to force a positive point of view onto people overwhelmed by frustration. It is about me as I struggle to have my knowledge of how to guide people who are stuck be subordinate to my desire to witness clients' own ability to guide themselves.

Right now, I am waiting for a young couple. I want to help them through an impasse in their relatively new and, they say, fortunate relationship. Keith is disturbed by unwanted and unsettling feelings about Colleen's previous relationships. I know a lot about such situations. This couple seems much better off in disposition and affection than many other couples. Their problems seem really to be Keith's problem, insecurity affected by millennia of male entitlement and possessiveness. But I am also aware that Colleen must bring her own inner and outer reactions to the process. I wonder whether this or that idea or technique would help them on their way. I also want to understand them as they have reflected on their own process and their reactions to our first session last week. Can I be simply interested in what they think and want and how they handle their own predicament? Can I be humble enough to let whatever purpose exists in the trouble they are having work its effect? Can I witness what they try to do and help them name their own unique feelings and concerns? Can I provide a climate in which they can learn?

Person-Centred Systems Therapy: Trust in the Process

I asked two colleagues when they knew they were a family therapist. My friend Larry Chamow, author (Patterson et al. 1998), teacher and experienced therapist, talked about starting out in his twenties in a shelter for runaway teenagers. He was simply asked to see a family instead of an individual. Not knowing anything about it except his experience with individuals and groups, he found himself not worried:

> I remember feeling very much at ease in the role as I think I had been doing this in my family for many years. My naïveté as to my role, goals and any real understanding was actually an asset.

Talking further, he said he was not anxious because he didn't feel responsible for the process and was comfortable with silence. He had no doubt that something would come from the family that would make the process work.

Breffni Barrett, therapist, teacher and former president of the California Association of Marriage and Family Therapists, said something similar:

> I was with a family of a teenager with many drug and other problems for whom several treatment programmes and expert efforts had failed. I felt helpless so I looked for the system to help. I noticed that her father looked so pale, shaken and frustrated that I was afraid he would have a heart attack in the session. So I turned to the girl and asked 'What are we going to do to keep your father from having a heart attack?' That got the conversation on a whole different track.

The system that was frustrated in trying to change and stop the young girl was ready to be positively activated when the problem was responding to her father's health danger. Seeing either of these two therapists now, their clients may gain from their years of experience, but perhaps benefit more from their confidence and trust in the process.

I have often had experiences with couples in which an impasse is followed by a significant event of one person reaching out in a way their partner was able to feel and respond to. I remember one frustrated woman running away from home. Her usually distant and self-absorbed husband went searching for her all over town and found her in a hotel, where they talked for hours, reconnected and let their frustrating teenage children fend for themselves for a night. One couple, usually loving, were working on what to do when one of them occasionally would 'lose it' and fall into a dark, negative mood for days and days. Recently, the other person fell into an angry, blaming mood for more than one day and had the experience of 'losing it'. Her sharing the experience of being lost and his original way of handling it in the direction of reconciliation and repair increased not only their closeness, but also their confidence that their problems were not insurmountable for a couple with their imagination and ability to love and that they were, in fact, nicely balanced.

The Guidance of Carl Rogers

Carl Rogers, the founder and inspiration for the person-centred approach, addressed the American Psychological Association annual meeting after receiving its lifetime achievement award. Reflecting on his long career, he articulated one central core position first described in 1945:

> I have come to trust the capacity of persons to explore and understand themselves and their troubles, and to resolve those problems, in any close, continuing relationship where I can provide a climate of real warmth and understanding. (Rogers 1980: 38)

Whether expressed in terms of a universal actualizing tendency or in the simple term 'trust the process', the person-centred approach begins and ends with attention to the client's ability to use resources if given an opportunity.

Rogers expected to find order and growth in each meeting and so he did. 'If you treat people as if they are trustworthy, they *are* trustworthy,' he said at the age of 80, reporting on how his career as a therapist shaped his career as a scientist (Berwick and Rogers 1983). 'He had too high an opinion of everything,' wrote an admiring friend in tribute to American philosopher and pioneering psychologist William James (Chapman 1991); Rogers has been compared to James (Wood 2008). Both are noted for scientific investigation embedded in experience as well as belief in the human capacity to change (Rogers 1980; James 1982). Rogers' optimism makes him highly compatible with the family therapy tradition of seeing the strength more than pathology (Hoffman 1998, 2002), good intentions instead of bad behaviour, unique outcomes (unexpected positive moments) rather than problem-saturated stories (White and Epston 1990).

In the same talk to the American Psychological Association, Rogers said the following:

> I can see what is perhaps one overriding theme in my professional life. It is my caring about communication. From my very earliest years it has, for some reason, been a passionate concern of mine. I have been pained when I have seen others communicating past one another. I have wanted to communicate myself so that I could not be misunderstood. I have wanted to understand, as profoundly as possible, the communication of the other, be he a client of friend or family member. I have wanted to be understood. I have tried to facilitate

clarity of communication between individuals of the most diverse points of view. (1980: 64–5)

A person-centred couple and family therapist does not claim that better communication, in itself, will free couples and families from problems and predicaments. They do assert, with Rogers, that therapists must seek to communicate as best they can – with congruence and careful empathy, not cleverness. For example, a 70-year-old Rogers was present while a group of therapists and consultants was painstakingly defining the many things wrong with one of its members, who, in turn, attempted without success to explain himself, defend himself and say what he had expected from the group. During a silence that came late in a very discouraging process, Carl said to the member: 'You are looking to be heard but all you are getting is feedback.'His words and manner not only described the group member's predicament, but also calmed everyone enough for a more useful exchange to take place. This incident reveals Rogers as therapist and person: his economy and accuracy with words and his ability to see the internal validity of a person's experience despite the agitation of the surrounding social field. Perhaps most importantly, it showed a person who practised this: pay close attention to an individual's experience rather than impose judgement no matter what. Relevant to relationship therapists, Rogers had the security not to get caught up in the intense social atmosphere and the humility to hold his position without blaming others in the room. He was about communication, rather than a focus only on his emotional reactions to a difficult situation.

Therapy for Rogers was not about what he could do for clients, but what clients, set free from an atmosphere of fear and rejection, could do for themselves. The client would be given as complete attention as possible for the purpose of learning, understanding, behaving more congruently or any other object that the client might have. Client-centred meant that there was no other centre – other people's expectations, the therapist's knowledge, a treatment plan worked out with a supervisor – than the clients' experience. 'The theory is the client,' says person-centred family therapist Ned Gaylin (2008). This attention, accompanied by acceptance and permission, applied to work with couples and families, can introduce systemic change. Box 8.1 describes the reflections of Lynn Hoffman, who included the experience of Carl Rogers in her *Family Therapy: An Intimate History* (2002).

Box 8.1: Carl Rogers' Example Observed by a Family Therapy Elder

Historian of family therapy and post-modern therapist Lynn Hoffman once described her experience of watching a film of Carl Rogers interviewing a young woman in 1984, when he was 82. Among her observations were these:

- 'He leaned toward his interlocutor as a sailor might lean into the wind, but remained nearly motionless as he questioned and reflected back. As a result, his style differed vastly from the impression left on me by phrases like active listening or unconditional positive regard.'
- Hoffman describes Rogers' many responses to his client's story: his guesses at her feelings based on her movements as much as her words and unsaid conclusions behind what she did say. For example, when she talks about not telling loved ones about a miscarriage, 'Rogers responded "That must be very hard." There was a long silence and Rogers didn't move. The woman finally said, "If you don't tell anybody you lost it, you lose it alone."'
- Rogers then said, 'You think, "Could I have done something differently? You were the keeper and you did lose it."' Hoffman tells of a long series of exchanges in which Rogers now offers reflections of her feelings, now articulates her self-accusations. Near the end of the interview, 'Rogers said, "it's a bodily feeling." She again said "Yes." He said "You're not really fulfilled." She said "Not completely." He said: "It's a real sadness."'
- 'At this point, there was a palpable shift. The woman suddenly went on a new tack, saying, "But some good things emerged. I saw a side of my husband that was strong." I was struck by the unexpectedness of the remark.' In the discussion with the audience after the interview, 'the woman said she had found it easy to talk with Rogers because she didn't feel she was being judged. Rogers said that at first he felt clumsy getting into her world ... Rogers said that his intention throughout was to be a companion to the woman in her own world, with the hope that she would feel released enough to go forward. She confirmed his observation saying, "I got in touch with the good parts when we were talking about failure." Second, in the words of the philosopher Jean-François Lyotard (1996) "he spoke in order to listen," as opposed to "listening in order to speak." Third, by joining the woman in her frustrations, Rogers may have amplified them until she finally let them go.'
- Hoffman concludes: 'Roger's video reminded me that the history of therapy contains many treasures buried in plain sight. We are often kept from using them because of an old feud in the field or because disciples have worn out the freshness of the ideas ... I found that his practices, including the way he embodied his words, resemble what I think of as a collaborative working style' (Hoffman 2002: 179–81). Hoffman's reflection integrates the spirit of Roger's example with the spirit of systems thinking in collaborative relationship therapy. Rogers way of being – companionship and joining as the heart of the work – is a model not of how to behave or how to use techniques, but of how to be as a therapist in the varying contexts in which we are asked to work.

Humility and Confidence

Carl Rogers' central principle was that the opportunity represented by the therapy hour was not the result of the therapist's knowledge and experience, but happened when the client was in the presence of that therapist's willingness, interest and ability to see and accept the world from that client's point of view.

In fact, therapist confidence has been linked to successful outcomes in several studies (Sprenkle et al. 2009). Sometimes, however, a lack of confidence can bring out my best. I can give myself the option of asking a colleague to help me focus. More often I write down: What is the situation? What are they likely to be coming for and how can I be ready for them? How can I prepare? And I do prepare some questions and ideas for myself. I am ready to invite conversation, 'speaking in order to listen', offering ideas on how they can communicate and connect with each other. My lack of confidence turns into thoughtfulness and readiness. Paradoxically, the more I am prepared to make sense of the therapy session and to invite clients into dialogue, the more I feel free to let the session take any shape that the clients want. Back to this little family: everyone gets a say; everyone defines the problem.

Who Needs the Person-Centred Approach?

I do when:

- The lessons I have to teach my clients overwhelm my desire to make sure I understand them.
- I find one client worthy of my attention and their partner, child or parent in need of my instruction.
- My words are beginning to be heard more often and at greater length than the clients'.
- My diagnosis of my clients makes the therapy hour seem more a predictable exercise than a meeting between persons.
- Nothing a person says could surprise me.
- Perhaps most importantly, I become overwhelmed that the clients' apparent problems seem much greater than their resources.

The experienced therapist needs the example of the direct, humble but confident Carl Rogers, who once told a client: 'it seemed that we had both tried, but we had failed and that we might as well give up our contacts'

(Rogers 1967). Recently, an evaluation by a client in couple therapy let me know that, five months after a mild confrontation that I had thought was worked through very well, he felt I understood how he felt 'very little'. It was the memory of Rogers that made me more interested in valuing that client's ability to be open now than to be defensive about his long silence.

The inexperienced therapist needs Rogers in order to remain confident that their receptivity, attention, respect and caring may be of more use to the client than the apparently greater authority and knowledge of the more experienced. Rogers commented with surprise on a study in which experienced therapists did not uniformly demonstrate empathy (1980: 148). I was recently contacted by one of my first clients 35 years after her therapy. She wanted me to know how helpful I had been and that her life had gone well. She told me: 'For a while you were all that kept me going.' I remembered her well; I especially remembered how unhelpful and incompetent I had felt.

Reflection on (or imagined supervision with) Rogers could increase the confidence of the inexperienced therapist and reduce the self-centred and exaggerated authority of the experienced therapist. The experienced therapist has to concentrate on meeting the clients as if they were their first, keeping at bay the tendency to finish clients' sentences, to blurt out elegant summaries of what they haven't even given them a chance to say, to introduce ideas they have not asked for and, especially, to make a diagnostic judgement that the client is unable to change. The inexperienced therapist needs confidence in the most important tools: their ability to join the client in a collaboration; to notice the details of clients' lives that can lead them out of their distress; and the patience to work with the client's unique reality rather than impose their own direction. The experienced therapist can replace the superiority of 'prior knowledge' (Goolishian and Anderson 1992) with the energy of alert exploration; the inexperienced therapist can channel the energy of fear of inadequacy into confident security that they already know what is most important: tuning in to the client's reality.

If Carl Rogers Were My Co-therapist for a Couple or Family

- I would be the more prepared and knowledgeable about the family situation; his preparation would be to focus his ability to enter the world of each person present.

- He would be respectful of me, curious about this medium of therapy, a good listener to me, to the clients and to himself. That respect would make me more thoughtful and trusting of the clients and of myself.
- As a person who rejected an instructor's traditional role with the parents he counseled when he worked in child (family) guidance in the 1930s (Rogers 1967), he would be convinced that listening to clients was the path to helpfulness.
- He would be uneasy if I were long-winded, careless in understanding clients on their own terms, directive, certain I knew best or judgemental. He would express himself to me if his uneasiness persisted. His way of doing this would be unlikely to put me on the defensive or feel attacked. As almost always, he would be speaking for himself rather than against me.
- After a bit of trying to be exactly like him, I would become more active, reframing the presenting problem in an inclusive way; acknowledging the silent; naming unspoken issues. I would take responsibility for a process that would facilitate uneasy people together in the room. I would rely on him to stay faithful to the process of carefully hearing whatever was said with complete attention.
- Sometimes the process would be best facilitated by my offering a perspective that allowed the family to engage with one another; sometimes the process would be saved by his unwavering patience and trust that clients would sort out their issues.
- He would offer a position of deep listening, attention and quiet expectancy; I would offer experience in putting people at ease, in reframing antagonism and blaming into the feelings that inform them, and in explanation of the possibilities of the meeting.
- He would sometimes wonder why this guy (me) was talking so much; I might think that this family won't even notice him if he doesn't speak more. I hope we both would listen to and be guided by what the clients say they want.

Of course, Carl Rogers is no longer with us and I (or you, the reader) am the one in the room with my clients. We can only be ourselves, who have learned from Carl Rogers and the many voices of couple and family therapists.

Case Example 8.1: Learning Empathy by Not Having to Have It

Rita, nervous about therapy and defensive, attended therapy only to save her marriage at her husband's insistence after he learned she had been having an affair. Her husband, Sam, was comfortable in therapy, open about his feelings of hurt and doubt, needing her to share openly her own feelings so that he could learn whether or not to trust her love for him. The therapist could only meet them both as they were.

THERAPIST: Sam doesn't want you to feel bad; he does, however, want you to know what he has been through.

RITA: I know, but I feel guilty anyway. All I can think about is how badly I hurt him.

THERAPIST: You're here because you care. But you can't feel good being here.

RITA: Yes. I'll keep coming because he wants me to but I can't feel anything but bad being here.

SAM: I don't want you to feel bad, I just need to know if you really want to be with me or you're just afraid to end the marriage.

THERAPIST: He's really wanting these meetings but can't feel good in them if you can only come because he is making you.

RITA: *(laughs)* That's the best I have right now.

The therapist continued through several sessions acknowledging that Rita's love was shown in her behaviour rather than in the expression of feelings her husband desired. At one point she said: 'Empathy! That's what he's always said I don't have. I never like to think about negative things. I just like to live life and enjoy it.' The therapist responded: 'You feel under pressure: like "I am supposed to have empathy now." But it doesn't feel natural, like you are trying to be someone you're not.' The therapist introduced topics – the story of their marriage (see Chapter 3) and the stories of their upbringing (see Chapter 6) – as ways to continue the conversation without remaining fixed on the impasse of their different views of the therapy.

After more than a dozen sessions (held about every two weeks), Sam spoke with strong feelings about the affects on his childhood happiness of his mother's affair and the subsequent divorce of his parents. Rita became tearful.

RITA: I feel for him. He's always the one. Always the one who feels every-thing; who gets hurt the most. He never wanted that to happen in his own life and here I am. I made it happen. I'm sorry.

SAM: I don't want you to be sorry. I just want you to understand how I feel.

RITA: Well, I do feel sorry and I do understand how you feel. It makes me sad. You had to live that way as a child and now you have to live that way in your marriage.

In later sessions, Rita was able to talk about her own feelings, frustra-tions with Sam and the way the marriage felt to her. She would intro-duce topics like: 'See, when he is staying up late writing in his journal and doesn't come to bed, I can't sleep. I want him to talk to me and tell me how he feels rather than writing. I would rather hear him even if I don't like what he has to say.'

Rita gradually became an active participant in the therapy that at first seemed like a punishment to her. The therapist's listening to and hearing her reluctance and valuing it as much as her husband's open sharing opened the door to her finding empathy that could be expressed in her own way.

'[I]n the interchange of the moment, I don't think my mind is filled with the thought of "Now I want to help you",' said Carl Rogers to philosopher Martin Buber. 'It is much more I want to understand you. What person are you behind that paranoiac screen or behind all these schizophrenic confusions, or behind all these masks that you wear in your real life? Who are you? It seems to me that is a desire to meet a person, not now I want to help. It seems to me that I've learned through my experience that when we can meet, then help does occur, but that's a by-product.' (Kirschenbaum and Henderson 1990: 55).

In his 1956 dialogue with B. F. Skinner (a famous meeting between the great behaviourist and the humanist, both eminent researchers and writ-ers), Rogers used Skinner's own writing as a path towards common ground between them:

I welcome being reminded of Dr. Skinner's very inspiring article in the *American Psychologist* on the processes of science as he had experi-enced them in his own career. As I remember that article, Dr. Skinner gives a very vivid picture of the scientific life as process. This is exactly the kind of thing that I have been trying to describe ... Far from knowing where he was going to come out, he had to live in process and had to let learnings emerge as they emerged, shaping his new behaviour. This makes me feel a great deal about Dr. Skinner, to realize that in his own life ... (Skinner laughs) in his own life he values that emerging unpredictable process. What I have been trying to say about the kind of culture I would want to design and the kind of outcomes I see in therapy when therapy is successful, is that it leads to exactly that kind of thing. The individual becomes an ongoing process of life in which the outcome is not set. There are no static goals. You don't even know if you will come out happy. You are living this on a day-by-day basis, endeavoring to be open to all of your experience. (Kirschenbaum and Henderson 1990: 144–5)

Person-centred couple and family therapists bring their whole selves, including their training, experience and knowledge of the way problems get resolved and predicaments clarified, to every meeting with clients. Their attention to the clients' own direction, expressed and implied, is at the heart of their work.

Case Example 8.2: Self-Actualization and a Facilitative Boy-Scout Troop

Half Dome in California is a mountaintop in Yosemite National Park, split cleanly in half by a glacier with a flat face rising straight up over 5000 feet above the Yosemite Valley floor. Climbers who ascend take as long as three days to do so and rest in sleeping bags hanging by ropes suspended over the valley floor. There is a back way that the common folk climb, still not very easy if you are at all fearful of heights. You hike up 10 miles and then you pull yourself up several hundred steep yards holding a steel cable that is nailed into the rock while your feet scramble on the too smooth rock. Other people climb down on the same cable, their feet sometimes sharing the same thin wood planks nailed into the rock several yards apart. Overcoming my fears and strong imagination in order to climb it was a great achievement for me, but that's not my story here.

When I was on top of the mountain, I started running into members of a young boy-scout troop. They had climbed Half Dome and were chattering about this and that, but especially one thing. 'Morgan is coming,' they were saying. As I headed down on the steel cable, I heard again 'Morgan is coming' as other boys passed me, clambering up past me. Again and again, 'Morgan is coming'. All these boys, it seemed to me, had expected themselves to be able to match wits with Half Dome and get up there despite the height and the effort, but Morgan was clearly different.

'Who is Morgan?' I reflected then and now. I felt that I knew Morgan without even ever seeing him. Morgan might be you or me, with something keeping him from what he might desire from life. Perhaps he felt that life did not equip him for what, it seems, everyone else could do without mishap. Morgan was someone who was not expected to climb Half Dome even though everyone else could. Perhaps he was timid, perhaps plagued by doubt or with physical or psychological reasons to hesitate in front of life's next challenge. Perhaps Morgan came from a harsh and sad family where no encouraging words were spoken. Whatever the reason, I had a picture that Morgan felt himself to be an unpromising person leading an unpromising life.

Yet here was the reality: Morgan was coming; something had happened in his favour. A facilitative boy-scout leader or troop? An encouraging friend? Or maybe some readiness that surprised him had made some new effort suddenly possible. As I went down the single cable from the top of the dome, I saw those beneath me seem one after the other to fling themselves out, almost to be suspended in mid-air as something small and round and red made its way up the cable without looking above or below at anything except the next handhold on the cable. Morgan was coming and Morgan had passed me and Morgan had climbed Half Dome. Morgan had climbed Half Dome!

Some combination of group spirit and inner readiness had allowed a new moment, surprising to all present. Something akin to the goals of a person-centred family therapy had occurred. A system had made a shift in the direction of promising change and I was glad to witness it.

Afterword

Clients have frustration, disappointment, hopelessness and a feeling of not knowing how to get on together. They also have histories of solving problems, accepting differences and the relief of a developmental crisis having passed. Couple and family therapy is a natural process following individual and collective stories until sources of stress are identified and possibilities for togetherness, letting each other alone and individual and collective action are opened.

'It is not what the person-centred approach gives you. It is what it does not take away,' said Carl Rogers, paraphrasing Gertrude Stein (O'Hara 2007). A person-centred therapist sees clients as resourceful, as actualizing or seeking to become their full selves, as worth listening to and, if heard and accepted on their own terms, capable of change that could not be predicted or even imagined if they felt not heard or accepted. A person-centred therapist, therefore, doesn't take away client autonomy, client intuition, client ingenuity and, especially, client self-acceptance and self-respect.

A family or couple therapist may be person centred even if they have never heard of Carl Rogers; at the same time, a therapist who has studied every word written about the person-centred approach needs to continually renew their commitment that the clients feel in charge of their own lives, respected, accepted and understood on their own terms. There is no guarantee that the therapist will trust the clients' ability to find their way, be guided by the clients' priorities or stay curious about what the clients want understood unless the therapist works on deepening these values.

I have sometimes asked students and colleagues: 'What kind of therapist would you allow to see your family of origin?' A very common answer is: 'Someone who is strong.' Asked to explain strength, people describe a quality of being able to allow each person space to be heard as well as the ability to facilitate safety from disrespect or rejection. Interestingly, respondents showed much concern for the apparently most dominating person in the group – father or mother, perhaps – that they would not shout down or shut down other people, but also that they would be able to preserve their self-respect.

The person-centred qualities I work to develop include responses to the three challenges with which I began this book:

- *Multi-directional partiality*: That ability to accept and seek understanding of each person present is the unvarying pathway to good therapy. Individuals feeling genuinely understood without having to cut off their intimate relationships opens the door to systems change. The therapist doesn't have the power to create intimacy, but shows its possibility by attitude and action. Carl Rogers' example was one of patient expectation: everyone can be understood, he seems to have thought, and because of that be liberated to move in a constructive direction.

- *Use of knowledge and skills*: The person-centred couple and family therapist is a student of relationship development. Families and couples always interact in the shadow of external conditions and internal patterns, which sometimes can be named in a safe, client-friendly environment. Therapists cannot and should not impose explanations for client troubles or solutions for distress; they can model curiosity about obstacles to connection and development that are not of clients' making. Good therapy widens vision and opens options.
- *Active facilitation*: Finally, an active facilitator allows external and internal permission for listening, acceptance, noticing of growth, change and effort to contribute. Couple and family therapy is a task for the clients, a person-to-person meeting for the therapist and an opportunity for all.

References

Abrams-Spring, J. (2005) *How Can I Forgive You? The Courage to Forgive, the Freedom Not To.* New York: Harper-Collins.

Anderson, H. (1997) *Conversation, Language and Possibilities: A Postmodern Approach to Therapy.* New York: Basic Books.

Anderson, H. (2001) Postmodern collaborative and person-centred therapies: What would Carl Rogers say? *Journal of Family Therapy* 23: 339–60.

Anonymous (1972) Toward the differentiation of self in one's own family. In J. L. Framo (ed.), *Family Interaction.* New York: Springer.

Anonymous (1978) The essence of being stuck: It takes one to think you know one or work on the therapists' own family. *International Journal of Family Counseling* 6(2): 36–41.

Asay, T. P. and Lambert, M. J. (1999) The empirical case for the common factors in therapy: Quantitative findings. In M. Hubble, B. L. Duncan and S. D. Miller (eds), *The Heart and Soul of Change: What Works in Therapy*, 33–55. Washington, DC: American Psychological Association.

Atkins, D. C., Dimidjian, S. and Christiansen, A. (2003) Behavioral couple therapy: Past, present and future. In T. L. Sexton, G. R. Weeks and M. S. Robbins (eds), *The Handbook of Family Therapy: The Science and Practice of Working with Couples and Families*, 281–303. New York: Brunner-Routledge.

Barrett-Lennard, G. T. (1998) *Carl Rogers' Helping System: Journey and Substance.* London: Sage.

Barrett-Lennard, G. T. (2005) *Relationship at the Centre: Healing in a Troubled World.* London: Wurr.

Beels, C. (2009) Some historical conditions of narrative work. *Family Process* 48: 363–78.

Bepco, C. and Johnson, T. (2000) Gay and lesbian couples in therapy: Perspectives for the contemporary therapist. *Journal of Marital and Family Therapy* 26(4): 409–20.

Berg, I. K. and Miller, S. D. (1992) *Working with the Problem Drinker: A Solution-Focused Approach.* New York: Norton.

Bernstein, A. C. (2000) Straight therapists working with lesbians and gays in family therapy. *Journal of Marital and Family Therapy* 26(4): 443–54.

Berwick, K. and Rogers, C. R. (1983) Keith Berwick and Carl Rogers. *At One With.* Los Angeles: NBC TV.

Blow, A. J. and Sprenkle, D. H. (2001) Common factors across theories of marriage and family therapy: A modified Delphi study. *Journal of Marital and Family Therapy* 27(1): 385–402.

Blow, A. J. and Sprenkle, D. H. (2007) Is who delivers the treatment more important than the treatment itself? The role of the therapist in common factors. *Journal of Marital and Family Therapy* 33(3): 298–317.

Blumstein, P. and Schwartz, P. (1983) *American Couples: Money, Work, Sex*. New York: Morrow.

Boscolo, L., Chechin, G., Hoffman, L. and Penn, P. (1987) *Milan Systemic Family Therapy*. New York: Basic Books.

Boszormenyi-Nagy, I., Grunebaum, J. and Ulrich, D. (1991) Contextual therapy. In A. S. Gurman and D. P. Kniskern (eds), *Handbook of Family Therapy, Volume 2*, 200–39. New York: Brunner/Mazel.

Bott, D. (2001) Client-centered therapy and family therapy: A review and a commentary, *Journal of Family Therapy* 23(4): 361–78.

Bowen, M. (1978) *Family Therapy in Clinical Practice*. New York: Jason Aronson.

Boyd, G., DeMarco, J. and Knowlan, A. (2000) Winter Course, American Academy on Physician and Patient. Burlington, VT.

Bozarth, J. D. (1984) Beyond reflection: Emergent modes of empathy. In R. F. Levant and J. M. Schlien (eds), *Client-Centered Therapy and the Person-Centered Approach*, 222–42. New York: Praeger.

Brown, L. S. and Zimmer, D. (1986) An introduction to therapy issues of lesbian and gay male couples. In N. J. Jacobson and A. S. Gurman (eds), *Clinical Handbook of Marital Therapy*, 451–71. New York: Guilford.

Burns, D. (2010) Presentation: Treatment of Anxiety. Denver, CO.

Butler, M. H. and Bird, M. H. (2000) Narrative and interactional process for preventing harmful struggle in therapy: An integrative empirical model. *Journal of Marital and Family Therapy*, 26(2): 123–43.

Butler, M. H., Davis, S. D. and Seedall, R. D. (2008) Common pitfalls of beginning therapist utilizing enactments. *Journal of Marital and Family Therapy* 34(3): 329–52.

Butler, M. H. and Gardner, B. C. (2003) Adapting enactments to couple reactivity: Five developmental stages. *Journal of Marital and Family Therapy* 29(3): 311–28.

Cain, D. J. (2010) *Person-Centered Psychotherapies*. Washington, DC: American Psychological Association.

Cecchin, G. (1987) Hypothesizing-circularity-neutrality revisited: An invitation to curiosity. *Family Process* 26(4): 405–13.

Chapman, J. J. (1991) William James. In J. Gross (ed.), *The Oxford Book of Essays*. Oxford: Oxford University Press.

Clark, W. M. and Serovich, J. M. (1997) Twenty years and still in the dark? Content analysis of articles pertaining to gay, lesbian and bi-sexual issues in marriage and family journals. *Journal of Marital and Family Therapy* 23(3): 239–53.

Cooper, M. (2008) *Essential Research Findings in Counseling and Psychotherapy*. London: Sage.

Cooper, M., O'Hara, M., Schmid, P. F. and Wyatt, G. (eds) (2007) *The Handbook of Person-Centered Therapy*. London: Palgrave Macmillan.

Cooper, M., O'Hara, M., Schmid, P.F. and Wyatt, G (eds) (forthcoming) *The Handbook of Person-Centered Therapy,* 2nd edn. London: Palgrave Macmillan.

Cornelius-White, J. (2007) Congruence. In M. Cooper, M. O'Hara, P. F. Schmid and G. Wyatt (eds), *The Handbook of Person-Centered Therapy.* London: Palgrave Macmillan.

Coulson, W. (1973) *A Sense of Community (Studies of the Person).* Columbus, OH: Merrill.

de Shazer, S. (1982) *Patterns of Brief Therapy.* New York: Guilford.

de Shazer, S. (1994) *Words Were Originally Magic.* New York: Norton.

Doherty, W. J. (1999) Divided loyalties: The challenge of step-family life. *Family Therapy Networker* May/June: 32–38, 54.

Donne, J. (1624) *Devotions on Emergent Occasions.* London.

Duncan, B. L. (2005) *What's Right with You?* Deerfield Beach, FL: Health Communications.

Duncan, B. L., Hubble, M. A. and Miller, S. D. (1997a) *Escape from Babel: Toward a Unifying Language for Psychotherapy Practice.* New York: Norton.

Duncan, B. L., Hubble, M. A. and Miller, S. D. (1997b) *Psychotherapy with 'Impossible' Cases.* New York: Norton.

Duncan, B. L. and Miller, S. D. (2000) *The Heroic Client: Doing Client-Directed Outcome Informed Therapy.* San Francisco: Jossey-Bass.

Falicov, C. J. (1986) Cross-cultural marriages. In N. J. Jacobson and A. S. Gurman (eds), *The Clinical Handbook of Marital Therapy*, 429–51. New York: Guilford.

Falicov, C. J. (2003) Culture in family therapy: New variations on a fundamental theme. In T. L. Sexton, G. R. Weeks and M. S. Robbins (eds), *The Handbook of Family Therapy: The Science and Practice of Working with Couples and Families*, 37–58. New York: Brunner-Routledge.

Farson, R. (1987) Dick Farson with the community. *Living Now Institute.* La Jolla, CA: Center for Studies of the Person.

Framo, J. L. (1992) *Family of Origin Therapy: An Intergenerational Approach.* New York: Brunner/Mazel.

Framo, J. L. (1996) A personal retrospective of the family therapy field: Then and now. *Journal of Marital and Family Therapy* 22(3): 289–316.

Freedman, J. and Combs, G. (1996) *Narrative Therapy: The Social Construction of Preferred Realities*. New York: Norton.

Friedman, E.. (1991) Bowen theory and therapy. In A. S. Gurman and D. P. Kniskern (eds), *The Handbook of Family Therapy, Volume 2*, 134–71. New York: Brunner/Mazel.

Gaylin, N. L. (1989) The necessary and sufficient conditions for change: Individual versus family therapy. *Person Centered Review* 4(3): 263–79.

Gaylin, N. L. (2001) *Family, Self and Psychotherapy: A Person-Centered Perspective.* Ross-on-Wye: PCCS Books.

Gaylin, N. L. (2008) Person-centred family therapy: Old wine in new bottles. *Person-Centered and Experiential Psychotherapies* 7: 235–44.

Goolishian, H. A. and Anderson, H. (1992) Strategy and intervention versus nonintervention: A matter of theory. *Journal of Marital and Family Therapy* 18(1): 5–15.

Gordon, T. (1970) A theory of healthy relationships and a program of parent effectiveness training. In J. T. Hart and T. M. Tomlinson (eds), *New Directions in Client-Centered Therapy*, 407–25. Boston, MA: Houghton Mifflin.

Gottman, J. M. (1989) Keynote address. *American Association of Marriage and Family Therapists Annual Conference*. San Francisco, CA.

Gottman, J. M. (1991) Predicting the longitudinal course of marriages. *Journal of Marital and Family Therapy* 17(1): 3–7.

Gottman, J. M. (1994) *Why Marriages Succeed and Fail … and How You Can Make Yours Last*. New York: Simon and Schuster.

Gottman, J. M. (1999) *The Marriage Clinic*. New York: Norton.

Gottman, J. M. (2009) Posting on a twelve year research project comparing gay and lesbian couples and cross-sex couples. Gottman Relationship Institute, www.gottman.com.

Gottman, J. M. and Gottman, J. S. (2007) *And Baby Makes Three*. New York: Crown Publishers.

Gottman, J. M. and Silver, N. (1999) *The Seven Principles for Making Marriage Work*. Three Rivers, MI: Three Rivers Press.

Gottman, J. M., Gottman, J. S. and DeClaire, J. (2006) *10 Lessons to Transform Your Marriage*. New York: Three Rivers Press.

Gottman, J. M., Levenson, R. W., Gross, J., Frederickson, B. L., McCoy, K., Rosenthal, L., Ruef, A. and Yoshimoto, D. (2003) Correlates of gay and lesbian couples relationship satisfaction and relationship dissolution. *Journal of Homosexuality* 45(1): 23–43.

Green, R.-J., Bettinger, M. and Zacks, E. (1996) Are lesbian couples fused and gay male couples disengaged? Questioning gender straightjackets. In J. Laird and R.-J. Green (eds), *Lesbians and Gays in Couples and Families: A Handbook for Therapists*, 185–230. San Francisco, CA: Jossey-Bass.

Greenberg, L. S. and Goldman, R. N. (2008a) *Emotion-Focused Couple Therapy: The Dynamics of Emotion, Love and Power*. Washington, DC: American Psychological Association.

Greenberg, L. S. and Goldman, R. N. (2008b) The dynamics of emotion, love and power in an emotion-focused approach to couple therapy. *Person-Centered and Experiential Psychotherapies* 7: 279–94.

Greenberg, L. S. and Johnson, S. M. (1986) Emotionally focused couples therapy. In N. S. Jacobson and A. S. Gurman (eds), *Clinical Handbook of Marital Therapy*, 313–17. New York: Guilford.

Guerney, B. G. (1977) *Relationship Enhancement*. San Francisco, CA: Jossey-Bass.

Haley, J. (1973) *Uncommon Therapy*. New York: Norton.

Haley, J. (1982) *Reflection on Therapy and Other Issues*. Chevy Chase, MD: Family Therapy Institute of Washington DC.

Haley, J. and Richeport-Haley, M. (2007) *Directive Therapy*. Bingingham, NY: Haworth Press.

Hoffman, L. (1998) Setting aside the model in family therapy. *Journal of Marital and Family Therapy* 24(2): 145–57.

Hoffman, L. (2002) *Family Therapy: An Intimate History.* New York: Norton.

Hubble, M. A., Duncan, B. L. and Miller, S. D. (1999) *The Heart and Soul of Change: What Works in Psychotherapy.* Washington, DC: APA Press.

Jacobson, N. S. and Christiansen, A. (1996) *Integrative Couple Therapy: Promoting Acceptance and Change.* New York: Norton.

James, W. (1982) *Varieties of Religious Experience*, ed. M. Marty. New York: Penguin.

Johnson, S. M. (2004) *The Practice of Emotionally Focused Couple Therapy*, 2nd edn. New York: Brunner-Routledge.

Johnson, S. M. (2008) Moment by moment: Getting to the heart of couple therapy. Psychotherapy Networker Conference, Washington, DC.

Johnson, S. M. and Greenberg, L. S. (1994) Emotion in intimate relationships: A synthesis. In S. M. Johnson and L. S. Greenberg (eds), *The Heart of the Matter: Perspectives on Emotion in Marital Therapy*, 297–325. New York: Brunner/Mazel.

Johnson, S. M. and LeBow, J. (2000) The coming of age of couple therapy: A decade review. *Journal of Marital and Family Therapy* 26(1): 23–38.

Kirschenbaum, H. (2007) *The Life and Work of Carl Rogers.* Ross-on-Wye: PCCS Books.

Kirschenbaum, H. and Henderson, V. L. (1989) *The Carl Rogers Reader.* London: Constable.

Kirschenbaum, H. and Henderson, V. L. (1990) *Carl Rogers: Dialogues.* London: Constable.

Kramer, P. (2002) Introduction to paperback edition of C. R. Rogers, *On Becoming a Person.* Boston, MA: Houghton Miflin.

Kurdek, L. A. (1998) Relationship outcomes and their predictors: Longitudinal evidence for heterosexual married, gay cohabitating and lesbian cohabitating couples. *Journal of Marriage and the Family* 60: 553–68.

Laird, J. (2000) Gender in lesbian relationships: Cultural, feminist and constructionist reflections. *Journal of Marital and Family Therapy* 26(4): 455–67.

Lambers, E. (2006) Supervising the humanity of the therapist. *Person-Centered and Experiential Psychotherapies* 5: 266–76.

Law, I. (1997) Attention deficit disorder; Therapy with a shoddily built construct. In C. Smith and D. Nylund (eds), *Narrative Therapies with Children and Adolescents*, 282–306. New York: Guilford.

Lerner, H. (1989) *The Dance of Intimacy.* New York: HarperCollins.

Lyotard, J.-F. (1996) *Just Gaming*, trans. W. Godzich. Minneapolis, MN: University of Minnesota Press.

Madanes, C. (1981) *Strategic Family Therapy.* San Francisco, CA: Jossey-Bass.

Madanes, C. (2009) Colorado Association of Marriage and Family Therapists Annual Conference, Denver, CO.

Madigan, S. (1994) The discourse unnoticed: Story-telling rights and the deconstruction of longstanding problems. *Journal of Child and Youth Care* 9(2): 79–86.

Madsen, W. C. (2007) *Collaborative Therapy with Multi-stressed Families*, 2nd edn. New York: Guildford.

McGoldrick, M. and Carter, B. (2001) Advances in coaching: Family therapy with one person. *Journal of Marital and Family Therapy* 27(3): 281–300.

McGoldrick, M. and Gerson, R. (1985) *Genograms in Family Assessment*. New York: Norton.

McGoldrick, M., Pierce, J. K. and Giordano, J. (eds) (1982) *Ethnicity and Family Therapy*. New York: Guilford.

McLeod, J. (2006) Relational depth from the point of view of the client. Presentation at the retirement conference of Professor Dave Mearns, University of Strathclyde, Glasgow.

McMillan, M. and McLeod, J. (2006) Letting go: The client's experience of relational depth. *Person-Centered and Experiential Psychotherapies* 5: 277–92.

Mearns, D. (1997) *Person-Centred Counselling Training*. London: Sage.

Mearns, D. and Dryden, W. (eds) (1989) *Experiences of Counselling in Action*. London: Sage.

Mearns, D. and Thorne, B. (1988) *Person-Centred Counseling in Action*. London: Sage.

Mearns, D. and Thorne, B. (2000) *Person-Centred Therapy Today: New Frontiers in Theory and Practice*. London: Sage.

Mearns, D. and Thorne, B. (2007) *Person-Centered Counseling in Action*, 3rd edn. London: Sage.

Miller, S. D., Hubble, M. and Duncan, B. (1995) No more bells and whistles. *The Family Therapy Networker* 19(2): 53–63.

Minuchin, S. (1974) *Families and Family Therapy*. Cambridge, MA: Harvard University Press.

Mitrani, V. B. & Perez, M. A. (2003) Structural-strategic approaches to couple and family therapy. In T. L. Sexton, G. R. Weeks, and M. S. Robbins (eds), *Handbook of Family Therapy*, 177–200. New York: Brunner-Routledge.

Moser, M. B. and Johnson, S. M. (2008) The integration of systems and humanistic approaches in emotionally focused therapy for couples. *Person-Centered and Experiential Psychotherapies* 7: 262–79.

O'Hara, M. (2007) Psychological literacy for an emerging global society: Another look at Rogers' 'persons of tomorrow' as a model. *Person-Centered and Experiential Psychotherapies* 6: 45–60.

O'Leary, C. J. (1989) The person-centered approach and family therapy: A dialogue between two traditions. *Person Centered Review* 4: 308–23.

O'Leary, C. J. (1999) *Counselling Couples and Families: A Person-Centred Approach*. London: Sage.

O'Leary, C. J. (2003) *Finding a Better Way to Feel Sorry for Yourself*. DVD. Wheat Ridge, CO: Denver Film and Digital.

O'Leary, C. J. (2008) Response to couples and families in distress: Rogers' six conditions lived with respect for the unique medium of relationship therapy. *Person-Centered and Experiential Psychotherapies* 7: 294–307.

O'Leary, C. J. and Johns, M. J. (2007) Couples and families. In M. Cooper, M. O'Hara, P. F. Schmid and G. Wyatt (eds), *The Handbook of Person-Centered Therapy*. London: Palgrave Macmillan.

Palazzoli, M. S., Boscolo, L., Chechin, G. and Prata, G. (1981) *Paradox and Counter-paradox: A New Model in the Therapy of the Family in Schizophrenic Transaction*. New York: Aronson.

Palmer, P. (1997) Presentation: American Association on Physician and Patient, Madison, WI.

Papp, P. (1983) *The Process of Change*. New York: Guildford.

Parker, P. (2000) For the white person who wants to know how to be my friend. In G. Anzaldua (ed.), *Making Faces, Making Soul: Hacienda cara*. San Francisco, CA: Aunt Lute Foundation.

Patterson, J., Williams, L., Grauf-Grounds, C. and Chamow, L. (1998) *Essential Skills in Family Therapy: From First Interview to Termination*. New York: Guilford.

Pittman, F. S. (1999) *Grow Up! How Taking Responsibility Can Make You a Happy Adult*. New York: Golden Books.

Rober, P. (1999) The therapist's inner conversation: Some ideas about the self of the therapist, therapeutic impasse and the process of reflection. *Family Process* 38: 209–28.

Rober, P. (2002) Constructive hypothesizing, dialogic understanding and the therapist's inner conversation: Some ideas about knowing and not-knowing in the family therapy session. *Journal of Marital and Family Therapy* 28: 467–78.

Rober, P. (2005) Family therapy as a dialogue of living persons: A perspective inspired by Bakhtin, Voloshinov and Shotter. *Journal of Marital and Family Therapy* 31: 385–99.

Rober, P. (2008) The therapist's inner conversation in family therapy practice: Struggling with the complexities of therapeutic encounters with families. *Person-Centered and Experiential Psychotherapies* 7(4): 245–61.

Rober, P. (2010) The interacting-reflecting training exercise: Addressing the therapist's inner conversation in family therapy training. *Journal of Marital and Family Therapy* 36(2): 158–70.

Rogers, C. R. (1957) The necessary and sufficient conditions of therapeutic personality change. *Journal of Counseling Psychology* 21(2): 95–103.

Rogers, C. R. (1959) A theory of therapy, personality and interpersonal relationships as developed in the client-centered framework. In S. Koch (ed.), *Psychology: A Study of a Science. Volume 3: Formulations of the Person and the Social Contract*, 184–256. New York: McGraw-Hill.

Rogers, C. R. (1961) *On Becoming a Person*. Boston, MA: Houghton-Mifflin.

Rogers, C. R. (1967) Autobiography. In E. W. Boring and G. Lindzey (eds), *A History of Psychology in Autobiography, Vol. V*, 343–84. New York: Appleton-Century-Crofts.

Rogers, C. R. (1969) *Freedom to Learn: A View of What Education Might Become*. Columbus, OH: Merrill.

Rogers, C. R. (1972) *Becoming Partners: Marriage and Its Alternatives*. New York: Delta.

Rogers, C. R. (1980) *A Way of Being*. Boston, MA: Houghton-Mifflin.

Salama, M. B. and Chou, C. (2009) Presentation at Winter Course. American Academy on Health Communication.

Satir, V. (1964) *Conjoint Family Therapy*. Palo Alto, CA: Science and Behavior Books.

Satir, V. (1972a) *Perceptions: The Personal Aspects of Therapy*. Videotape. Boston, MA: Boston Family Institute.

Satir, V. (1972b) *People-Making*. Palo Alto, CA: Science and Behavior Books.

Schmid, P. F. (2002) Knowledge or acknowledgement? Psychotherapy as 'the art of not knowing' – Prospects on further development of a radical paradigm. *Person-Centered and Experiential Psychotherapies* 1(1/2): 56–70.

Schmid, P. F. (2004) Back to the client: A phenomenological approach to the process of understanding and diagnosis. *Person-Centered and Experiential Psychotherapies* 3(1): 36–51.

Schmid, P. F. (2006) The challenge of the other: Towards dialogical person-centered psychotherapy and counseling. *Person-Centered and Experiential Psychotherapies* 5(4): 240–54.

Schwartz, R. (2002) *The Skilled Facilitator: A Comprehensive Resource for Consultants, Facilitators, Managers, Trainers and Coaches*, 2nd edn. San Francisco, CA: Jossey Bass.

Seaburn, D. (2007) Therapy with kids, parents and schools: A collaborative approach. Psychotherapy Networker Symposium, Washington, DC.

Scheiffer, H. (2008) Presentation at Psychotherapy Networker Symposium, Washington, DC.

Senge, P. (1990) *The Fifth Discipline: The Art and Practice of the Learning Organization*. New York: Doubleday.

Sexton, T. L., Ridley, C. R. and Kleiner, A. J. (2004) Beyond common factors: Multilevel-process models of therapeutic change. *Journal of Marital and Family Therapy* 30(2): 131–50.

Sexton, T. L., Weeks, G. R. and Robbins, M. S. (2003) *Handbook of Family Therapy*. New York: Brunner-Routledge.

Shernoff, M. (2006) Negotiated non-monogamy and male couples. *Family Process* 45(4): 407–18.

Shotter, J. (1993) *Conversational Realities*. London: Sage.

Simon, R. (2007) The top ten. The most influential therapists of the past quarter-century. *The Psychotherapy Networker* 31(2): 24–37, 68.

Smith, C. and Nylund, D. (eds) (1997) *Narrative Therapies with Children and Adolescents*. New York: Guilford.

Sprenkle, D. H. and Blow, A. J. (2004a) Common factors and our sacred models. *Journal of Marital and Family Therapy* 30(2): 113–32.

Sprenkle, D. H. and Blow, A. J. (2004b) Common factors are not islands – they work through models: A response to Sexton, Ridley and Kleiner. *Journal of Marital and Family Therapy* 30(2): 151–8.

Sprenkle, D. H., Davis, S. D. and Lebow, J. L. (2009) *Common Factors in Couple and Family Therapy: The Overlooked Foundation for Effective Practice*. New York: Guilford.

Stuart, R. B. (1980) *Helping Couples Change: A Social Learning Approach to Marital Therapy*. New York: Guilford.

Stuart, R. B. and Jacobson, B. (1987) *Couple's Therapy Workbook*. Champaign, IL: Research Press.

Taffel, R. (1991) How to talk with kids. *The Family Therapy Networker* 15(4): 3846, 6870.

Taffel, R. (2001) *The Second Family*. New York: St Martin's Press.

Taffel, R. (2005) *Breaking Through to Teens*. New York: Guilford.

Taffel, R. (2008) Walking the line: Doing concurrent individual and family therapy with teens and their parents. Psychotherapy Networker Conference, Washington, DC.

Treadway, D. (2008) Behind closed doors: When couple's therapy doesn't improve sex. Psychotherapy Networker Conference, Washington, DC.

Visher, E. B. and Visher, J. S. (1982) *How to Win as a Step-family*. New York: Brunner/Mazel.

Visher, E. B. and Visher, J. S. (1987) *Old Loyalties, New Ties: Therapeutic Strategies with Step-families*. New York: Brunner/Mazel.

Warner, M. S. (2007) Client incongruence and psychopathology. In M. Cooper, M. O'Hara, P. F. Schmid and G. Wyatt (eds), *The Handbook of Person-Centered Therapy*, 154–67. London: Palgrave Macmillan.

Weingarten, K. (1995) Radical listening: Challenging cultural beliefs for and about mothers. In K. Weingarten (ed.), *Cultural Resistance: Challenging Beliefs about Men, Women and Therapy*, 2–22. Binghamton, NY: Blackwell.

White, M. (2007) *Maps of Narrative Practice*. New York: Norton.

White, M. and Epston, D. (1990) *Narrative Means to Therapeutic Ends*. New York: Norton.

Wile, D. (1993) *After the Fight: A Night in the Life of a Couple*. New York: Guilford.

Wood, J. K. (2008) *Carl Rogers' Person-Centered Approach: Toward an Understanding of Its Implications*. Ross-on-Wye: PCCS Books.

Wylie, M. S. (1994) Panning for Gold. *Family Therapy Networker* (18)6.

Wylie, M. S. (2004) Mindsight. *Psychotherapy Networker* 28: 29–39.

Index